THE WESTERN BAHR AL-GHAZAL
UNDER BRITISH RULE: 1898-1956

T0289526

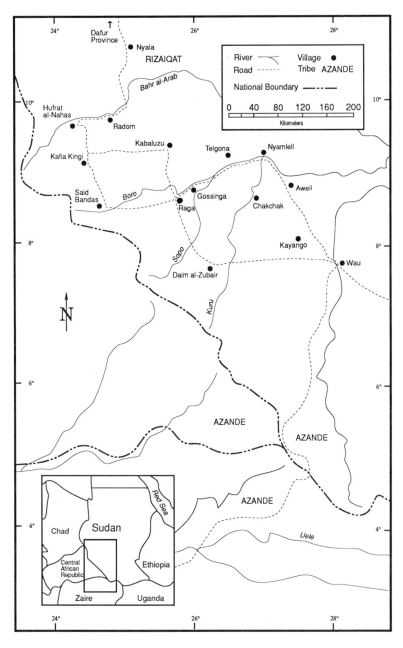

Sketch map of Western Bahr al-Ghazal Province showing
some towns, roads and tribes.

THE WESTERN BAHR AL-GHAZAL
UNDER BRITISH RULE: 1898-1956

by

Ahmad Alawad Sikainga

Ohio University Center for International Studies
Monographs in International Studies

Africa Series Number 57
Athens, Ohio 1991

© Copyright 1991 by the
Center for International Studies
Ohio University

Printed in the United States of America
All rights reserved

The books in the Center for International Studies Monograph
Series are printed on acid-free paper ∞

Library of Congress Cataloging-in-Publication Data

Sikainga, Ahmad Alawad.
   The western Bahr al-Ghazal under British rule, 1898-
1956 / by Ahmad Alawad Sikainga
   p.   cm. – (Monographs in international studies.
Africa series; no. 57.)
   Includes bibliographical references and index
   ISBN 0-89680-161-6
   1. Bahr al-Ghazal (Sudan : Province) – History. 2.
Sudan – History –1898-1956.
       I. Title. II. Series.
DT159.6.B34S55   1991
962.4–dc20   90-41421
                                                    CIP

CONTENTS

TABLES

PREFACE

Initial research for this study was undertaken in 1984-1985 and the findings were submitted as a doctoral dissertation for the University of California at Santa Barbara in 1986. The principal sources were contemporary British and Sudanese archives. These were supplemented by oral material collected in 1987. More exhaustive work in the South was hindered by the then-current civil war in the region. I hope that this study will stimulate further research in the history of this remote and yet important part of the Sudan.

In transliteration, I have used the modern literary Arabic form without diacritical marks. One of the principle problems in doing this is the spelling of names of people and places. In the spelling of northern Sudanese personal and place-names, I have preferred to use the classical Arabic form rather than the European corruption. In the spelling of southern Sudanese names, I have used the classical Arabic form when the name is clearly derived from Arabic, an example is Daim al-Zubair instead of Deim Zubeir. On the other hand, I have used the conventional form when the place or personal name is derived from a local source. The appendices were written in colloquial Arabic. Their translation, therefore, required some flexibility.

The present study was made possible through the help of a number of institutions and individuals. The original research was undertaken with the aid of generous grants from the Ford Foundation and the University of California at Santa Barbara. I am grateful to the directors and the staff of the following archives: the National Record Office, Sudan; the Public Record Office, Sudan; the Sudan Archives of Durham University; and the School of Oriental and African Studies of London University. It is a pleasure to offer my appreciation to professor Robert O. Collins who supervised the original dissertation, not only for his keen scholarly counsel, but also his sustaining help and encouragement. An expression of gratitude is also due to professors Wesley Johnson and Nancy Gallagher who read the original manuscript. Many thanks go to Dr. Martin Daly whose comments have saved me from many errors. Finally, I would like to thank Ms. Arlene Puentes of Hunter College, City University of New York and Ms. Peggy Satler of Ohio University for their help with the map. The views expressed in this study remain the responsibility of the author alone.

INTRODUCTION AND A NOTE
ON THE SOURCES

In the broadest sense this study examines the nature of contacts between the inhabitants of the middle Nile valley and their southern neighbors in northern Equatorial Africa and the transformation of their relationship under European colonial rule. Specifically, the enquiry focuses on the policies of the British colonial administration in the western Bahr al-Ghazal in the southwestern corner of the republic of the Sudan.

Western Bahr al-Ghazal or "Dar Fertit" is perhaps one of the least known places in Africa. Yet this remote and isolated area can be regarded as a historical barometer, registering major developments in the history of the Nile valley. In the nineteenth century, the region became one of the most active slave-exporting zones in Africa. The name "Dar Fertit" itself conjures up images of conquest and enslavement and evokes the activities of al-Zubair Pasha Rahma and the slave traders. In the twentieth century, however, western Bahr al-Ghazal became a laboratory in which the British colonial administration applied one of its most controversial policies in the Sudan, the so-called Southern Policy.

This study is mainly about the colonial phase of the history of the western Bahr al-Ghazal. The history of British administration in this part of the southern Sudan is significant in many ways. It is common knowledge that the colonial period holds a central position in the history of sub-Saharan Africa's relationship with the world economy. European territorial expansion either "opened up" whole regions for the first time, or else intensified the process of capitalist penetration of African societies. Very little is heard, on the other hand, of those places where several decades of colonial rule failed to establish any significant links with the world economy. Southern Sudan in general and western Bahr al-Ghazal in particular fall within this category. By all the yardsticks of "development" (cash economy, industrialization, wage-employment, formal education and so forth), western Bahr al-Ghazal can be regarded as a Cinderella.

Historical migration, contacts with the Muslim north, and the nineteenth-century slave trade led to the spread of a veneer of Muslim influence and an Arabic pidgin that distinguished this area from the rest of the South. Consequently, the region was viewed by British officials as a Muslim enclave in the non-Muslim South and became the target and test of the Southern Policy.

The Setting

The western Bahr al-Ghazal is a vast territory. It is bounded by the Bahr al-Arab to the north, Dinka land to the east, Azande country to the south, and the Central African Republic to the west. The region consists of plains, intersected by numerous streams which turn into impassable swamps during the rainy season, creating an environment suitable for the spread of the tsetse fly. Hence agriculture has remained the basic means of subsistence. Traditionally, inhabitants practiced a system of production based on seasonal shifting cultivation of grains such as sorghum and varieties of millet. The primary aim of production was subsistence which was often supplemented by hunting, fishing, and gathering. Since the nineteenth century, elephant tusks and ostrich feathers were sought for payment of tribute to local rulers and for long-distance trade. Nonetheless, the area has very few resources and inhabitants have always fallen prey to famine and disease.

The inhabitants of this remote part of the Bahr al-Ghazal represent a convergence of different ethnic and linguistic groups speaking varieties of eastern and central Sudanic languages. They include the Kreish, Feroge, Binga, Kara, Yulu, Nyagulgule, Dango, Belanda, Bviri, Sere, Ndogo, and Golo, among many others. In addition to these there are numerous immigrants from west Africa, such as the Hausa, Borno, and Fulani, and from Chad, the Central African Republic, and the northern Sudan. The whole region for the most part has a low population density. Arable land is extensive. Small groups often have split from larger ones to clear land and found settlements which shifted frequently to avoid attacks from powerful neighbors. This fractionalized assemblage of people had never formed a unified political entity and had often fallen prey to external aggressions. Yet, despite the absence of large-scale political units, several factors such as long-distance trade and external pressures did contribute to the rise of a centralized authority among groups such as the Feroge, Nyagulgule, Kreish, Binga, Kara, and Yulu. One of the most striking aspects of the history of these groups is the prevalence of a migration tradition. As a result of constant external pressures these peoples have been on the move for at least two centuries. The tradition of the Binga relates that they had once lived in the vicinity of Shala, a location confirmed by al-Tunisi in the nineteenth century. To the southwest lived the Yulu who spoke a language closely related to that of the Binga. Like their neighbors' their tradition indicates that they paid tribute to Darfur from 1800 onward. With the growing frequency of slave raids, they moved farther south in the decade that followed.[1] The tradition of the Kara, a people whose language resembles Binga and Yulu, suggests that they also once lived farther north and migrated southward to avoid slave raids. Similarly the oral history of the Kreish suggest a southward movement from their early location in southern Darfur. Threatened by further raids they continued to move to the south and southwest in the late nineteenth century. When they appeared to pose a threat to the newly-founded sultanate of Dar al-Kuti, Sultan Muhammad al-Sanusi began to send armed bands to attack their settlements. Many Kreish fled back to the east; others were captured and sold or incorporated into the population of Dar al-Kuti. Following the destruction of Dar al-Kuti by the French in 1911, a large number of the Kreish returned to the Sudan. Today, almost all of them live in the western Bahr al-Ghazal in which they became the largest ethnic group.

---

[1]Dennis Cordell, *Dar al-Kuti: A History of the Slave Trade and State Formation on the Islamic Frontier in Northern Equatorial Africa (Central African Republic and Chad) in the Nineteenth and Early Twentieth Century* (Ph.D. dissertation: University of Wisconsin, Madison, 1977), p. 37.

A very dynamic situation, however, existed in the northern and northwestern parts of the province, just to the south of the Bahr al-Arab which divides this area into two zones. To the north, the majority of people identify themselves as Muslims; to the south, Muslims are much less numerous. The presence of Muslim influence in the western Bahr al-Ghazal and the eastern Ubangi-Chari (Central African Republic) is a by-product of migration, historical contacts with the north, and the nineteenth-century slave trade. Another characteristic of the riverine demarcation line along the Bahr al-Arab was the existence of large-scale political units such as Darfur and Wadai. These empires possessed standing armies equipped with large numbers of European weapons. For the most part, the southern societies tended to be fragmented, relying for self-defence upon small kin-based levies of warriors armed with traditional weapons.

In order to understand the history of this part of the Bahr al-Ghazal, it is important to examine the way in which it was linked to the north and the pattern of interaction between the two regions. The rise of a large state in Darfur early in the seventeenth century, its role in the trans-Saharan trade, and its internal economy all encouraged the extraction of resources such as copper, ivory, and slaves from the southern hinterlands. Slaves, obtained through barter and official raids south of the Bahr al-Arab, played an important part in the economic and political life of the Fur sultanate. The story of the Darfur slave trade is well documented and has been dealt with elsewhere;[2] here it will be stressed that since the economy of the empire had become so closely linked to the southern peripheries, successive rulers of Darfur employed several mechanisms to assert their influence there. These included selection of suitable rulers who were capable of collecting tribute, trading facilities, and the bestowing upon them of traditional Fur titles such as *maqdum* and sultan. The most eminent vassals of Darfur in the western Bahr al-Ghazal were the ruling families of the Feroge, Nyagulgule, Binga, Kara, and some sections of the Kreish. This patron-client relationship is

---

[2]R.S. O'Fahey, "Slavery and the Slave Trade in Dar Fur," *Journal of African History* 14 (1973): 29-43.

well depicted in the oral traditions of both sides. From Darfur's perspective, this vast area was divided into a number of *shartayat* (chiefdoms), each was ruled by a *shartay* subordinate to the Aba Diimang or "lord of Diima," meaning the governor of the southern part of the sultanate.[3] It is not entirely clear whether these southern lands constituted a formal part of the kingdom of Darfur, but they undoubtedly lay within its recognized sphere of influence. The oral traditions of the southern people themselves lend support to this assumption. Several groups such as the Feroge, Nyagulgule, Binga, Kara, and some sections of the Kreish assert their subordinate status to Darfur in the past; the ruling families trace authority to the Fur sultans.

Political domination, raiding, enslavement gave rise to elaborate, racially pejorative vocabularies among northerners in regard to the south, and to assumptions of inferiority and superiority reinforced by religious criteria and presumptions of northerners' superior descent. Thus, inhabitants of the western Bahr al-Ghazal and the Chari Basin have been known historically to northerners as Fertit. This was a generic name used by the people of Darfur to describe the non-Muslim and stateless societies of the southern regions. As a label associated with subordination and enslavement, "Dar Fertit" was not so much a place as a state of mind; as the slave raiders moved southward "Dar Fertit" was pushed farther south. Several versions of Fur oral traditions describe the origin of the Fertit. According to one account, the Fur and Fertit have a common origin; they were descendants of twin brothers known as "Fir" and "Firat." The children of Firat have scattered and became Fertit. A more Islamically-colored version indicates that the Fertit were the original inhabitants of Jabal Marra, the heart of the Fur sultanate, and after the Islamization of the sultanate were forced to move south and split into several sections such as the Binga, Kara, Shaiu, Indiri, and Yulu.[4]

---

[3]R.S. O'Fahey, "Fur and Fartit: The History of a Frontier" in *Culture History in the Southern Sudan*, ed. John Mack and Peter Robertshaw (Nairobi: 1982), p. 78.

[4]Stefano Santandrea, *A Tribal History of the Western Bahr al-Ghazal* (Bologna: 1964), p. 144.

The Bahr al-Arab region was not only a field of economic exploitation but also an area where ethnic and social transformation took place. Within this frontier zone ethnic lables fluctuated in response to political exigencies. The ruling families of some groups such as the Feroge were upgraded from the inferior status of Fertit to that of *ahrar*, "free."[5] The Feroge were among the most loyal clients of Darfur. Their ruling family claimed descent from a Borno pilgrim who, in one version, settled in these lands on his way home from Mecca. The pilgrim is said to have gained the favor of the local ruler of the Kaligi, married his daughter, and eventually succeeded him. The Nyagulgule also trace their origin to the Bego of Darfur. Thus, formation of these small-scale political units followed a Sudanic paradigm: newcomers expel or absorb the indigenous population, with Islam as an ideological variable in the process. In the Sudanic belt the process of state formation has been associated with the legend of the "Wise Stranger." The Wise Stranger usually was said to be a Muslim holy man who came from a remote land, introduced Islam, often married the daughter of a local leader, and consequently bequeathed the right to rule to his descendants. While such claims to foreign origin are highly improbable, they nevertheless subsume a nexus of real events and a complex history. The prevalence of migration traditions among the ruling families and the important role they play as social charters implies substantial fluidity in social and political relationship. These legends were part of an elaborate strategy for political and economic control, because the ability to form genealogies which emphasized "superior" descent ostensibly led to positions of power and authority. While the historicity of such traditions may be questioned, they certainly give clues to the pattern of political transformation in this region.

Several trends influenced the history of the southern region during the nineteenth and twentieth centuries. These include the temporary technological and military advantages enjoyed by bands of European, Middle Eastern, and northern Sudanese slave

---

[5]Within the western Bahr al-Ghazal, the term Fertit was applied by Muslim groups such as the Feroge to non-Muslim groups such as the Kreish and Banda.

traders; the Mahdist invasions of in the 1890s; and finally the arrival of the European powers at the turn of the century. The first two will be discussed in the first chapter; the last constitutes the bulk of this study. Before examining the effects of these developments, a survey of the historical literature on the region is essential.

Sources

The peculiar geographic, social, and demographic characteristics of the western Bahr al-Ghazal and its fluid ethnic and linguistic situations render the task of reconstructing its history an unyielding enterprise. The inhabitants consist of multifarious ethnic and linguistic groups, most of whom were recent arrivals; each community developed a unique history and experience. In addition to this, nineteenth-century slave raids resulted in the dispersion and division of people, a situation further compounded by the general population transfer carried out by the Anglo-Egyptian government in the 1930s in line with its Southern Policy. Thus it is extremely difficult to write an integrated history that encompasses all the various ethnic groups in this vast area.

In the absence of a substantial body of indigenous written material, the history of the western Bahr al-Ghazal can be based only on a somewhat heterogeneous collection of sources, both written and oral. As far as the pre-colonial period is concerned, the only available sources consist of European travelers' accounts and of oral traditions.

While the Sahelian and Sudanic states of Darfur and Wadai were visited by a number of European and Muslim travelers, the Southern hinterlands never were reached by any of those explorers before the middle of the nineteenth century. Both Nachtigal and al-Tunisi, who visited Darfur and Wadai in the eighteenth and nineteenth centuries respectively, made only casual references to Dar Fertit as a major source of slaves and other commodities.

After the opening of the waterways of the White Nile in the middle of the nineteenth century under the aegis of the Turco-Egyptian regime, many European, Levantine, and northern Sudanese merchants and officials of the colonial government entered the South. They observed and reported on aspects of the region's life. Of unique significance as far as the western Bahr al-Ghazal was concerned were the works of two German botanists and explorers, Georg Schweinfurth (1836-1925) and Wilhelm Junker (1840-1892). In 1864 Schweinfurth came to Egypt, whence he traveled along the Red Sea coast from Qusair through Swakin to Massawa and then via Kassala, Gallabat, and Abu Haraz to Khartoum, collecting botanical specimens. In 1868 he made a second journey to the Sudan. From Khartoum he ascended the White Nile and Bahr al-Ghazal, reaching Azande country, and penetrated the hitherto unexplored regions of the southwestern Sudan and the Uele basin in 1870-1871. He then returned north by way of the Rohl River and Dar Fertit. Schweinfurth's best known work is *Im Herzen von Afrika*, translated into English as *The Heart of Africa*. From his accounts a detailed picture of the Bahr al-Ghazal during the era of the slave trade can be constructed.

Junker came to Egypt and made his way to the Sudan where he explored the lower reaches of the river Sobat and the western tributaries of the upper White Nile in 1876-1878. In 1879 he returned to the Sudan again to explore the region of the Congo-Nile watershed. He spent four years among the Azande and Monbuttu peoples. Trapped by the Mahdist revolt, Junker returned through Uganda and Zanzibar and arrived in Europe in 1887 carrying with him Amin Pasha's journals. His book, *Travels In Africa*, contains valuable information about the people of this area and their social organization.

Other books exist which give information about Bahr al-Ghazal during the latter half of the nineteenth century. One important work of this period is *Uganda and the Egyptian Soudan*, by the two missionaries Charles Wilson and R.W. Felkin. After a visit to Uganda they returned via the Bahr al-Ghazal in the late 1880s. Additional insights may be gained from the works of the Italian Gaetano Casati (1838-1902), who was employed as a topographer by Romolo Gessi in 1880. Casati explored the region of Wau, and the Azande and Monbuttu contries. In 1883 he traced the upper course of the river Uele. His account was published in a volume entitled *Ten Years in Equatoria*. Gessi's own book, *Seven Years in the Soudan*, gives a vivid description of his struggle against the slave traders and their activities. The writings of travelers during the latter half of the nineteenth century were influenced by historical developments in the region and consequently the slave trade became the dominant theme. Some of their accounts are marred by melodramatic, stereotypical, and emotional generalizations. Moreover, these works focused on the activities of the slave traders; less attention was given to the myriad effects of the slave trade and the response of the local people.

Some information on the history of the southwestern Sudan during this period may also be gleaned from books and reports in other European languages on neighboring lands that came under the domination of the Belgians and French. These include Daigre's *Oubangui-Chari*; De Calonne-Beanfait's *Les Azande*, and Auguste Chevalier's *L'Afrique Central Francaise, Recit du Voyage de la Mission*. During the Mahdiyah, Karamallah al-Kurkusawi and al-Khatim Musa led two expeditions to the Bahr al-Ghazal. They sent several reports which were included in the correspondence of Mahmud Wad Ahmad to the Khalifa.

For the colonial period, a very important genre consists of the reports, memoranda, and letters of British administrators in the South. Condominium officials left a substantial body of literature which describes the day-to-day affairs of the administration. It is usually not the officials of the first twenty years who provide the best insights into conditions of the South, but the administrators of the last thirty years or so. During the first two decades of this century the British presence in the South was tenuous and nominal. Those were the years of pacification and resistance. The Western District of the Bahr al-Ghazal was regarded as a hardship area and no British official wanted to be assigned there. It is not surprising, therefore, that the first twenty years of British rule are characterized by few reports and little official correspondence. The later generation of British administrators, who stayed longer in the area, were expected to have proficiency in indigenous languages and to study local customs. Of those officials G.K. Hebbert was a vivid example as far as the western Bahr al-Ghazal is concerned. He compiled a great deal of information and ethnographic data on the various groups in the area in the late 1920s. An extremly valuable source for the history of this part of the South is the work of Muhammad Abd al-Rahim, the Sudanese historian who was a *mamur* in Kafia Kingi in 1925-1926. His private collections are deposited in the National Records Office in Khartoum.

The greatest body of literature on the condominium was written during the heyday of the Southern Policy from 1930 until the time of independence. In addition to provinical files in the National Records Office, the private papers of some important district commissioners who served in the Western District such as J. Macphail, S.R. Simpson, D.J. Bethell, and D.M. Evans, are deposited in the Sudan Archive of Durham University.

Still there are limitations to the use of administrative documents no matter how detailed they are. There were some aspects of southern traditional life which administrators did not fully investigate. This gap in the official documents can be filled only by oral testimony. In this respect, most notable are the efforts of Father Stefano Santandrea, the Catholic priest who spent some thirty years in the western Bahr al-Ghazal and developed an intimate knowledge of the area and its people. During this period he compiled dictionaries and collected oral traditions. His collections were published in several books, of which *A Tribal History of the Western Bahral-Ghazal* and *Ethno-Geography of the Bahr al-Ghazal*, are of great value. In addition he published numerous articles in *Sudan Notes and Records*, *The Messenger*, and *Nigrizia*. Santandrea's works offer a wealth of information about the histories and cultures of various ethnic groups in the western Bahr al-Ghazal. However, Santandrea was concerned mainly with the identification of "tribes" and his works do not provide a historical chronology. Moreover, one must guard against the confusion caused by conflicting testimonies. This stems from the fact that local people tended to give different versions of their histories when faced with compulsory movement from one area to another. These traditions may be tested against other versions that were gathered by the later generation of British administrators. Thus, only by combining written and oral sources as well as by utilizing linguistic evidence, can the pre-colonial history of Dar Fertit be reconstructed.

Chapter 1

WESTERN BAHR AL-GHAZAL IN THE NINETEENTH CENTURY

Arguably the most important factor that shaped the history of the western Bahr al-Ghazal and adjacent regions was their integration into the trans-Saharan trade and the southward military and commercial expansion of Egypt in the nineteenth century. The copper mines of Hufrat al-Nahas attracted merchants from northern Sudan, Borno, and the Hausa trading states. As early as the eighteenth century, individual merchants, usually *jallaba* (traveling merchants) established commercial links with the local people in this area. They exchanged beads for ivory and slaves. Trading centers were established at Kafia Kingi, Said Bandas, Telgona, and Kabaluzu.[1] Between the seventeenth and the nineteenth centuries, the Fur sultanate emerged as the major political power in the western parts of the Nilotic Sudan with a recognizable sphere of influence that extended beyond its boundaries. The internal economy of the state and its position in the trans-Saharan trade required the integration of the southern hinterlands from which ivory and other commodities as well as slaves were procured. Slaves played a significant role in the economic and political life of the sultanate. For example, they were to be found as eunuchs, in the military, and as agricultural laborers. Slaves were obtained from the south through barter, and frequent organized raids were undertaken by enterprising

---

[1]Robert O. Collins, "Sudanese Factors in the History of the Congo and Central West Africa in the Nineteenth Century" in *Sudan in Africa*, ed. Yusuf Fadl Hasan (Khartoum: Khartoum University Press, 1970), pp. 160-61.

individuals under contract with the state. However, the Fur hegemony over the southern lands was challenged by new developments in the middle Nile valley in the mid nineteenth century. The Turkish conquest of the Funj sultanate in 1821 marked the beginning of a distinctive epoch in Sudanese history. It represented the first large-scale effort to draw the Nilotic regions into the expanding capitalist economy. The main objective of the new regime was mobilization of the natural and human resources of the newly-conquered territory. This could be achieved through taxes, duties, and concessions. With so much emphasis on commercial exploitation it was natural that the colonial government came to play a leading role in this process. Since one of the primary objectives of the conquest was to facilitate formation of a new slave-based army for Muhammad Ali, the Turco-Egyptian regime became the main slave recruiting organization. Moreover, increasing demand for ivory in Europe had spurred trade exploration and the opening of the White Nile waters for navigation in the early 1840s. Successive waves of European, Middle Eastern, and northern Sudanese traders rushed to the South. Eager to appropriate the resources of these virgin lands, these traders dominated the region by combining military power, political alliances, and the judicious organization known as the *zariba* system.[2] The new urban centers such as Khartoum became seats of foreign merchants who employed numerous Sudanese as servants, soldiers, game hunters, sailors, agents, and partners.

The Organization of the White Nile Trade

The merchants, known to Southerners as Khartoumers or *Bahara*, carved out most of the southern region and divided it into spheres of trade among themselves. Each trading house in Khartoum established a number of zaribas scattered over a wide area. These zaribas were usually built in the vicinity of a local community. A monopoly system was developed; once a group

---

[2]Richard Gray, *A History of the Southern Sudan 1839-1889* (London: Oxford University Press, 1961), pp. 58-69.

founded a zariba and entered into a trade relationship with local communities, it automatically had a monopoly in the area.[3] The Bahr al-Ghazal region was divided among six trading-houses in Khartoum and about half-a-dozen smaller trading-groups associated with them. The eastern part of the province was dominated by Europeans such as John Petherick, Alphonse de Malazac, and Ambrose and Jules Poncet. In the central and western parts of the Bahr al-Ghazal, however, non-Europeans prevailed. They included Ali Abu-Ammuri who established his zariba among the Bongo; Ginawi, an Egyptian, whose settlements stretched as far as the Welle River in the Congo; and Busili who established a series of zaribas throughout the Kreish and the Golo lands. Other traders in the region included the Aqqad brothers, Kuchuk Ali, Idris wad Daftar, and Arbab al-Zubair Adlan.

Initially, local chiefs were able to control the markets very much to their advantage. A good example is chief Guju of the Kreish-Ndogo who presided over a lucrative cattle market in his territory. However, after the arrival of the Khartoumers, Guju lost his wealth and prestige and became an ordinary man.[4] Several factors contributed to the shifting of power in favor of the traders. First, their companies were larger, wealthier, and had better access to resources than the old jallaba. Second, they possessed greater military capabilities which enabled them to build independent bases of power by incorporating slave troops in their armed bands. Finally, the Khartoumers formed alliances with local headmen whereby the latter provided the subsistence needs of the settlements in return for luxury goods, support in internal power struggles, and military assistance against external aggression.[5]

At the beginning the merchants were mainly interested in ivory which was in great demand in Europe for piano keys and billiard balls. Ivory was exchanged for beads, ostrich feathers, and other imported goods. However, demand for these commodities

---

[3]Gray, *History*, pp. 58-69.

[4]Georg Schweinfurth, *The Heart of Africa* (New York: Harper, 1874), vol. 2, p. 380.

[5]Gray, *History*, pp. 57-80.

was limited and traders were soon facing the problem of a decrease in the supply of ivory. Their solution was disastrous for large parts of the South. There was one article for which demand in the region was virtually unlimited–cattle. If the traders could supply cattle, ivory would be forthcoming. By playing on ethnic differences and establishing alliances with specific groups, the traders could get cattle in exchange for military support of their allies. An increasing part of the trader's capital, therefore, was invested in armed bands. The cost of maintaining these growing private armies threatened the profitability of the ivory trade. The traders tried to solve the problem by paying their soldiers in locally-captured slaves.[6] Indeed, the use of slave labor was not unknown among the local people. Domestic slavery was common among the Azande and the Dinka. However, the slave raids of the Khartoumers had no precedent in the region's history. There was a demand for slaves in the northern Sudan, Egypt, Arabia, and other parts of the Middle East. Very soon, slaving became the Khartoumers' main activity. And in this respect the zaribas came to play a major role in facilitating the exploitation of human and natural resources of the South.

The Structure of the Settlements

Violence was the dominant form of interaction between the merchants and local people during this phase of contact. However, once local resistance was suppressed the merchants proceeded to establish permanent settlements that led to a variety of relationships with the inhabitants. Each zariba was surrounded by a community of local people in a state of virtual vassalage to the zariba owners. They cultivated and supplied the food and served as bearers on the annual expeditions. In this manner, thousands of people were alienated from their traditional way of life and forced to serve the zariba owners.

---

[6]Gunnar Haaland, "The Jellaba Trading System" in *Trade and Traders in the Sudan*, ed. Leif O. Manger (Bergen: University of Bergen, 1984), pp. 269-84.

These zaribas resembled small towns with a heterogeneous population and a highly stratified social structure. At the top were the zariba's owners who were mainly European, Levantine, and northern Sudanese. Below them were the *wkala* (agents) who had proven organizational or military abilities and gained the confidence of the Khartoumers. A very important category were the jallaba whose presence in the region predated the Turkiyya. Although there were a few Greeks and Syrians, the majority of the jallaba were northern Sudanese, mainly Danaqla, Shaiqiyah, and Ja'liyyin. Their number increased after the establishment of the zaribas. The jallaba acquired slaves by bringing into the region a host of commodities that found ready markets in the zaribas. Another major component of the settlements were the merchants' armies. In order to ensure the continuous acquisition of slaves, the Khartoumers used two categories of soldiers: the *'asakir* and the *furukh*. The 'asakir were drawn from the Danaqla and Shaiqiyah and other groups from the northern Sudan. They were provided with firearms and served as guards to protect the settlements, escort the trading caravans, and conduct the *razzias* (raids) for slaves.[7] Although many found adventure in the South, very few found fortune. The 'asakir's pay was usually in the form of cloth, cattle, and other goods. These goods were often bartered with the jallaba for the necessities of life. The most profitable undertaking, from their point of view, were the razzias from which they received a large portion of the booty. Nevertheless, the 'asakir were almost continuously in debt to the wkala who overcharged them for goods. The 'asakir often owned a small number of slaves. While most of these slaves were to be sold, a few were kept for domestic purposes. The furukh, on the other hand, were drawn from among the local people. They formed the backbone of the merchants' armies; and generally were regarded as being the best soldiers. On an expedition, the furukh acted as flankers and scouts and were usually assigned the most dangerous tasks.

The merchant armies were divided into banners headed by officers from the northern Sudan or slaves who had risen from the ranks and gained the confidence of the Khartoumers. Thus the

---

[7]Schweinfurth, *Heart of Africa*, vol. 2, pp. 322, 427.

Bahr al-Ghazal became a training ground for the future Mahdist armies. A large number of these soldiers joined the Mahdist movement and played a major role in its success. Among those who rose to prominent positions were Hamdan Abu Anja and Zaki Tamal.[8]

In addition to these elements, small groups of Muslim religious *fakis* (religious teachers) came to reside in the settlements. They accompanied expeditions and acted as arbitrators and consultants on religious matters. These fakis preached Islam and converted a few Southerners to Islam.

By and large slaves formed the backbone of the settlements' population. While all the able-bodied were sold into slavery or recruited into the armies, women were used as domestic servants or concubines in the households of the merchants, the wkala, the jallaba, and the soldiers.

The local population were attached to the settlements and became a major source of their laborers, carriers, interpreters, and craftsmen. A system of forced labor emerged. Bongo blacksmiths, for instance, made the manacles and chains which were used in the slave raids and accompanied the expeditions to work bars of copper. Moreover, local people bore the additional burden of producing food for the settlements. Food production had been greatly decreased by the early depredation of the Khartoumers. Schweinfurth broadly divided the settlements' population into two social categories: a consumer class which included the Khartoumers and other foreign elements, and a class of producers that consisted of the local people.[9]

These settlements or *dium* (sing. *daim*) resembled cells into which people of diverse backgrounds were integrated. When Schweinfurth visited the area he wrote: "Ethnographically considered, Dar Farteet [sic.] presented a wondrous medley, perhaps no where else in an area so limited, could there be found such a conglomeration of representatives of different races as upon

---

[8]Interview with Madawi Abu Matariq, 28 June 1897.

[9]Schweinfurth, *Heart of Africa*, vol. 2, p. 322.

the cultivated tracts in the environs of the Dehms [sic.]."[10] They formed the nucleus for the growth of present-day Wau, Daim al-Zubair, and Daim Idris which were obviously named after the zariba owners. Their ethnic heterogeneity is reflected in the present-day composition of their population. Competition between Sudanese and European merchants was keen. However, measures taken by the colonial administration had tipped the balance in favor of non-European merchants. Such measures included attempts to monopolize trade, the imposition of heavy duties on both exports and imports, and the establishment of check points along the White Nile. While foreign firms were far more vulnerable to the caprices of the government, local traders who did not rely so much on river transport expanded their old trade routes across Darfur and Kurdufan. From the late 1860s onward, European traders began to leave and their stations were taken over by Levantines and northern Sudanese.[11] In addition to the desire for profits, the influx of northern Sudanese traders into the South was prompted by certain policies imposed by the colonial government in regard to taxation, land tenure, and commerce. In the first place, the colonial system of land tenure had led to large-scale accumulation of private property and resulted in a spectacular fractionalization of land in the northern Sudan.[12] As a result, thousands of peasants sought alternative careers such as in trade and the military. They left for Darfur, Kurdufan, and the southern regions which were yet to be brought into the orbit of the Turkish administration. These dreaded northerners played a major role in the economic exploitation of the South.

---

[10]Schweinfurth, *Heart of Africa*, p. 366.

[11]Anders Bjorkelo, "Turco-Jallaba Relations 1821-1885" in *Trade and Traders in the Sudan*, ed. Leif O. Manger (Bergen: University of Bergen, 1984), pp. 81-108.

[12]Jay Spaulding, "Slavery, land tenure and social class in the Northern Turkish Sudan," *International Journal of African Historical Studies* 15 (1982): 1-20.

Al-Zubair's Empire in the Bahr al-Ghazal

These stern times produced a number of men who, by harnessing and controlling the dynamic forces of the epoch, were able to prosper and rise to prominence at the expense of others. Some of them were self-made individuals from remote areas in the northern Sudan. They are best exemplified by al-Zubair Rahma Mansur who made use of every new trading, political, and military skill that came to hand and gave a special twist to the history of the Bahr al-Ghazal. Al-Zubair first entered the Bahr al-Ghazal in 1856 under the service of Ali Abu-'Ammuri. This first trip opened his eyes to the vast riches of the province and two years later he came to stay permanently. His first contact was with the Golo in the western part of the province. From there al-Zubair proceeded to Azandeland where he concluded a trading agreement with King Tikima and married one of his daughters.[13] At this stage of his career al-Zubair was just another trader among many and had to depend on the good will of local leaders. But he could hardly be satisfied with this position and conceived a much bigger role for himself; a role that could not be achieved without military power.

Al-Zubair then began to make every possible effort to raise an army. By 1859 he had amassed a force of four hundred men, most of whom were recruited locally. Tikima was alarmed and consequently al-Zubair was forced to leave Azandeland.[14] Al-Zubair was now convinced that he could no longer depend on the voluntary acceptance of the local leaders. The first casualty of the new strategy was Abu Shaka, the Golo chief who was killed in revenge for the murder of al-Zubair's brother.[15] However, the continuous hostility of the Golo forced al-Zubair to move his headquarters to the left bank of Khor Uyjuku in the land of the Kreish Ndogo. This station came to be known as Daim al-Zubair.

---

[13]For more details on the life of al-Zubair see H.C. Jackson, *Black Ivory: The Story of El-Zubeir Pasha Slaver and Sultan* (Oxford: Blackwell, 1913) and Sa'd al-Din al-Zubair, *Al-Zubair Rajul al-Sudan* (Cairo: 1952).

[14]Al-Zubair, *Al-Zubair Rajul*, pp. 40-42.

[15]Al-Zubair, *Al-Zubair Rajul*, pp. 40-42.

The strategic location of Daim al-Zubair was a contributing factor to his success: all the trade routes to the north passed through it. Al-Zubair reinvested a large portion of his profits in men and guns. By the mid 1860s his army numbered twelve thousand soldiers, known as *bazingers*. These men were equipped with modern firearms and became instrumental in his conquest of the province. The army was divided into banners headed by al-Zubair's kinsmen and other northern Sudanese. However, the supreme military command was placed in the hands of Rabih Fadl Allah, an adventurer from the Gezira region who later played a major role in the history of central Bilad al-Sudan.[16] In 1866 Zubair concluded a favorable treaty with the Rizaiqat of southern Darfur which gave him safe passage upon the payment of an agreed toll. By this he gained control over the trade route that passed through Darfur and Kurdufan to the north. The security and facilities that al-Zubair created, encouraged hundreds of traders to descend from Darfur, Kurdufan, and the riverine regions of the Sudan. In 1870 alone, it was estimated that several thousand jallaba traveled through Daim Zubair.[17] The village of Shaka in the Rizaiqat territory grew into a large intrepot in its own right and became an assembly point for caravans.

Al-Zubair's hegemony over the Bahr al-Ghazal remained unchallenged until the arrival of al-Hilali, a Moroccan who established an ascendancy over Hufrat al-Nahas. He was recognized by the sultan of Darfur as the ruler of the Bahr al-Ghazal on payment of an annual tribute. In 1869 al-Hilali was appointed governor of the province by the Turkish government. Al-Zubair refused to submit to the newcomer and eventually a confrontation took place in which al-Hilali lost his life. After eliminating this rival, Al-Zubair turned against Tikima who was subdued after thirteen months of fighting. Al-Zubair then proceeded to punish the Rizaiqat for breaking the treaty and attacking his caravans. The colonial government had no choice but

---

[16]W.K.R. Hallam, *The Life and Times of Rabih Fadi Allah* (Devon: Arthur Stockwell, 1979).

[17]Schweinfurth, *Heart of Africa*, vol. 2, p. 257.

to accept the fait accompli and in January 1874, Zubair was appointed governor of the Bahr al-Ghazal. At the end of the year he dealt a final blow to the Fur sultanate which was promptly annexed by the Turkish government.

Al-Zubair's commercial network now radiated from his headquarters at Daim al-Zubair to the Congo Basin in the south, and to Darfur in the north. Extensive mining was undertaken at Hufrat al-Nahas. The magnitude of al-Zubair's operations was unequalled among other traders. In 1870 a single expedition into the Bahr al-Ghazal came back with 120 hundredweight of ivory (which realized E£2,000 in Khartoum) and approximately two thousands slaves.[18] It is not entirely clear how much of his income was generated from the selling of slaves. In his memoirs, Zubair argued that he was procuring slaves for military purposes.[19] But these memoirs were written at the beginning of this century when slavery had already become a public issue.

The traders' activities were not limited to the mere capture and export of slaves but permeated every aspect of life in these territories and probed deeply into their social and political fabric. The large-scale use of modern technology such as boats, steamers, well-organized armies, and most important the large-scale use of firearms, had decisively transformed the balance of power in favor of the traders and gave them a tremendous advantage over small-scale and stateless societies. The merchants employed various techniques to gain economic and political control over the indigenous population. Those rulers who opposed or resisted were removed and replaced by loyal ones.

Indeed, one of the most important effects that has to be taken into consideration in assessing the impact of slavery is its demographic aspect. Unfortunately, the lack of reliable statistics makes it difficult to estimate the total population loss. However, it is evident that many areas were abandoned as a result of warfare and famine. When the first British officials arrived in this region at the beginning of this century, they were struck by its low

---

[18]Hallam, *Life and Times*, p. 40.

[19]Al-Zubair, *Al-Zubair Rajul*, p. 63.

population density. It was reported that al-Zubair alone exported about 1,800 people annually and that during the period 1857-1879, between eighty thousand and one hundred thousand were taken from Bahr al-Ghazal alone.[20] However, it is important to consider that not all the captives were exported and large numbers were absorbed into merchants' armies or kept by the Baqqara in southern Darfur and Kurdufan.

On another level, the traders' operations affected the pattern of population movement in the region. As the raiders struck from the north and the east, the major population drift continued toward the south and the southwest. This was indeed the case of the Binga, the Kara, the Banda, and the Kreish.

Although the traders reigned supreme in the region for more than two decades, their interests came into conflict with those of the colonial government. In an attempt to bring the upper Nile under control, the Turco-Egyptian regime began to take practical steps to abolish slavery. One of the methods adopted was the employment of European officers such as Samuel Baker and Charles Gordon. Although they were able to curtail the slave trade along the White Nile by establishing check points, they were unable to control the overland routes across Kurdufan and Darfur. However, the military campaign of Romolo Gessi dealt a serious blow to the traders. After executing Sulayman al-Zubair, Gessi expelled many jallaba and closed down the zaribas.

Despite the destruction of the power of the traders, their legacy remained. They initiated a process that persisted throughout the nineteenth and the early twentieth centuries. After the departure of the traders a number of individuals who were part of the traders' network rose to fill the power vacuum. They included local leaders, ex-slaves, and soldiers who replicated the methods of the Khartoumers by employing large armies; they expanded the enslavement frontier farther west to the Ubangi Chari. The most vivid example was Rabih Fadl Allah, an ex-slave who had become one of al-Zubair's leading generals. After Sulayman's death, Rabih re-assembled the remaining soldiers and raided the Kreish-Ndogo and the Aja. Threatened by the government, he moved west and

---

[20]Gray, *History*, pp. 58-69.

attacked the Banda for captives to be incorporated into his army or exchanged for arms. From there Rabih's conquest engulfed the Chad region and brought him to the eastern marches of Hausaland and the Borno kingdom which he eventually destroyed.[21]

Before leaving the Chari Basin, Rabih installed Muhammad al-Sanusi as sultan of Dar al-Kuti in the upper Ubangi-Chari. With the firearms initially acquired in 1891 after the massacre of the French expedition sent to his sultanate, al-Sanusi and his followers began extensive raiding among the Banda, Kreish, Yulu, and Sara peoples. He took advantage of links already established with the trading network of the north and began to export slaves and ivory in exchange for cloth, arms, and other luxury goods.[22] Once again, the people of the western Bahr al-Ghazal and the eastern Ubangi Chari had fallen prey to the system of institutionalized insecurity and disorder which continued until the beginning of the twentieth century.

Besides Rabih and al-Sanusi, there were many other warlords. They included al-Nur Angara, one of al-Zubair's lieutenants, who established a zariba among the Yulu and raided the local Banda, Golo, and Kreish. Many local leaders such as Surur and Rafai of the Zande and Bandas Hakim of the Kreish began to build their own bases of power.[23] They were helped by the influx of firearms which flowed into the region in ever-increasing numbers. Thus the official suppression of the slave trade was not accompanied by any diminution in the level of warfare in these remote lands. The whole region was riven by the ambitions of competing leaders such as Zemo of the Azande who led several campaigns against the people of the western Bahr al-Ghazal. Thus,

---

[21]For more details on Rabih's career see R.A. Adeley, "Rabih Fadallah, 1879-1893: Exploits and impact on political relations in Central Sudan," *Journal of the Historical Society of Nigeria* 5 (1979).

[22]Cordell, *Dar al-Kuti*, pp. 58-80.

[23]Dennis Cordell, "Warlords and Enslavement: A sample of slave raiders from Eastern Ubangi-Shari, 1870-1920" in *Africans in Bondage, Studies in Slavery and Slave trade*, ed. Paul Lovejoy (Madison: University of Wisconsin, 1986), pp. 335-65.

the disorder initiated by the Khartoumers continued over an ever-expanding zone that eventually extended beyond the Bahr al-Ghazal region.

The standard historiography of the Nilotic slave trade reflects an external perspective. Most writing on the subject tends to focus on the activities of the slave traders and the organization of the trade itself. The main source materials are travelers' accounts. The historical records of the local people consist largely of oral traditions. Although these traditions do not provide a complete picture of this important epoch, they do indicate the general reaction to the invaders. For the most part, people responded by either fleeing to the inaccessible forests and mountains, or putting themselves under the protection of powerful leaders. These turbulent days are still alive in their memories.

The Golo were one of the first people to encounter al-Zubair. At the beginning their chief welcomed him. But after the latter's return from Azandeland in 1864, he eliminated Kayango, the Golo chief at the time, for failure to perform according to al-Zubair's expectations. Perhaps one of the groups most affected by the traders' operations in the western Bahr al-Ghazal were the Kreish. Although they were the largest single ethnic group in the area the Kreish were divided into three sections: Kreish-Ndogo at Daim Zubair, Kreish-Naka at Said-Bandas, and Kreish-Hufra at Hufrat al-Nahas. The Ndogo section were the first to encounter al-Zubair. After the elimination of their chief, they were subdued and came to form the backbone of the settlement. They were able to rid themselves of the merchants' hegemony during Gessi's campaigns. The Kreish-Ndogo joined the government forces in hunting the jallaba. The Kreish-Hufra had paid tribute to the Fur sultan in the past. Casting an eye on the rich minerals of Hufrat al-Nahas, Al-Zubair raided the area and captured many people.[24] Most of the captives were taken to Daim al-Zubair and absorbed as bazingirs. They were not able to return to Hufrat al-Nahas until after the elimination of Sulayman. Afterwards, their ruling family was embroiled in conflict over the

---

[24]N.R.O. Bahr al-Ghazal Province 1/3/12 Notes on the Western District Tribes, 1927.

leadership of the group. One faction appealed to the Binga of Kafia Kingi and the other sought the help of the Ta'isha. The whole group was victimized by the Binga for several years. Finally, the Kreish Hufra appealed to the Naka clan, defeated the Binga and united their scattered people under Sultan Murad Angraib.[25] The history of the Naka section during this period resembles that of the Hufra and Ndogo clans. They had once lived in the Nile-Chari divide and paid tribute to the Fur sultan. They were able to put up a considerable resistance against al-Zubair. It was only after he combined his forces with Idris wad Daftar that he was able to defeat them and establish two settlements in their land: Njara and Njogo. The Naka revolted and killed al-Zubair's *wakil* and fled to Ndele in the eastern Ubangi-Chari. Over the next decade they developed a powerful political entity under the leadership of Bandas, a former bazingir of Idris wad Abtar. Bandas Hakim formed an alliance with the Aja and raided the small tribes of the border region. However, after the rise of al-Sanusi in Dar Kuti, Bandas led his followers to the Sudan at the beginning of this century where he was settled west of Raga.[26]

Further west two rivals of al-Zubair, Al-Dabi and Abu-Mangur established their settlements among the Binga, Kara, and Yulu. Al-Zubair was unwilling to allow any rivalry and he despatched al-Nur Angara to destroy these settlements. In the process a large number of locals were either killed or taken as captives. Even Muslim groups such as the Feroge and Nyagulgule did not escape the depredation. At first the Feroge sultan collaborated with al-Zubair but this collaboration soon turned into hostility when al-Zubair attempted to control him. An expedition led by Al-Nur Anqra was sufficient to break his power and the sultan was forced to flee to Darfur.[27] Al-Zubair then invaded Darfur and sent the Feroge back to the Bahr al-Ghazal. The fate of the Nyagulgule was no different. Their chief, Andal, was not on good terms with al-Zubair and he offered his support to a rival

---

[25]N.R.O. Bahr al-Ghazal Province 1/3/12.

[26]N.R.O. Bahr al-Ghazal Province 1/3/12.

[27]N.R.O. Bahr al-Ghazal Province 1/3/12.

merchant in Darfur. When al-Zubair invaded Darfur to eliminate his rival, Andal was captured and beheaded. He was succeeded by his son who made his headquarters in Telgona. It is not surprising, therefore, that the Nyagulgule offered considerable support to Gessi. They were supplied with firearms and were able to prevent the jallaba from passing through their land.[28]

It is evident that the later part of the nineteenth century in the Bahr al-Ghazal presents an almost apocalyptic picture of people fleeing and taking refuge in the bushes and mountains. In this respect the history of the Kreish, Binga, and Kara becomes a tale of continuous flight and disorder.

Although violence was the dominant form of interaction between the traders and the local people, slower processes were also at work. The presence of large numbers of Arabic-speaking Muslims and their intensive interaction with the locals led to the rise within the settlements of several Arabic pidgin-creoles that eventually spread to many parts of the South. Nevertheless, despite the presence of Muslims in the zaribas, there appears to have been no large-scale proselytization. Islam proved not to be a motivating factor behind trade activities. Although Islam theoretically prohibits enslavement of a Muslim, the few local Muslims did not escape enslavement. The role of the nineteenth-century Khartoumers and jallaba in the southern Sudan should not be compared with that of the Dyula traders who became the main agents of Islamization in West Africa. The majority of the traders in the South were migrant peasants from the northern Sudan trying to escape the ruinous taxation of the government. Their major concern was pillage rather than religious proselytization. Yet some of these individuals perceived their actions in normative frameworks. When al-Zubair first arrived in the Bahr al-Ghazal, he wrote to the Fur sultan asserting that the inhabitants of these lands were "heathens" who had no "master." Al-Zubair sought a religious justification for his actions, and even boasted that he ruled his empire on the basis of the " Quran and the Sunna" and brought peace and justice to this remote land which was sunk in "darkness, barbarism, and anarchy." In the eyes of the proponents of the Islamization of the

---

[28]N.R.O. Bahr al-Ghazal Province 1/3/12.

South, al-Zubair was a reformer who brought the people of the Bahr al-Ghazal into the realm of Islamic civilization. Writing on the same subject, Abbas Ibrahim said:

> This process of "Arabization" and "Islamization" seemed to have gained considerable momentum especially in Bahr al-Ghazal when Gordon embarked upon his policy of dispersing the "Arab" element and thus halting the process. Had Gordon not hurried the "northern" and, especially Zubair's troops, the process would have gone away to destroy many of the differences which helped and help to create and complicate the Southern problem.[29]

The Mahdists and the Europeans in the Western Bahr al-Ghazal, 1883-1898

When news of the Mahdist revolt reached the Bahr al-Ghazal, many rulers perceived it as an opportunity to rid themselves of the oppression of the colonial regime. Consequently, many went to offer their allegiance to the Mahdi and returned to the Bahr al-Ghazal accompanied by Mahdist agents.[30] In 1882 Sultan Yangu of the Nyagulgule allied with Madibu Ali of the Rizaiqat and led a revolt against the government in Telgona.

Toward the end of 1883, the political situation in the northern Sudan took a serious turn. The Mahdists won one of their most decisive battles at Shaikan. The Mahdi was now free not only to march on Khartoum, but also to send an expedition to

---

[29]Abbas Ibrahim Muhammad Ali, *The British, The Slave Trade and Slavery in the Sudan, 1820-1881* (Khartoum: Khartoum University Press, 1972), p. 144. See also Al-Zubair, *Al-Zubair Rajal*, p. 63 and *Al-Siyasah al-Talimiyah wa al-thagafa al-Arabiyah fi janub al-Sudan* (Khartoum: African Islamic Institute, 1983), pp. 11-12.

[30]Two of the local leaders, Musa Hamid of the Feroge and Hajar Dahiyah of Nyagulgule, went to al-Ubbayid and offered their allegiance to the Mahdi and returned to the Bahr al-Ghazal with Karamallah al-Kurkusawai.

the Bahr al-Ghazal. Consequently, he appointed Karamallah Muhammad Kurkusawi to the position of *amir* of the Bahr al-Ghazal and sent him with a large force to occupy the province. Karamallah followed the same tactics of the Khartoumers by establishing alliances with some local headmen and eliminating those who opposed him. As a result of Feroge and Nyagulgule agitation and the military might of Karamallah, Lupton Bey, an Englishman and last Turko-Egyptian governor of the Bahr al-Ghazal, surrendered the province on 28 April 1884.

Relations between the *Ansar* (the followers of the Mahdi) and local leaders began to deteriorate as a result of the former's raids for ivory and slaves and their attempts to capture Baqqara fugitives. As mentioned earlier, the local leaders supported the Mahdist revolution because they saw it as an opportunity to rid themselves of the colonial government. But when they realized that their independence was threatened by the Ansar they turned against the Mahdiya. It was discovered later that the Feroge sultan had supported anti-Mahdist rebels in Darfur, and his territory became a sanctuary for those who escaped from Mahdist rule.[31]

The Mahdist occupation of the Bahr al-Ghazal was short-lived. Following the Mahdi's death in June 1885, Karamallah was recalled by the Khalifa Abdullahi, the Mahdi's successor, to Umdurman. Karamallah's short reign in the Bahr al-Ghazal was marked by a high level of violence. He eliminated all those leaders who resisted and captured many of their subjects.

After the Mahdist withdrawal, the Bahr al-Ghazal witnessed another invasion. This time the threat came from the South, from the Avungara Zande. In 1890 Zemo began to advance northward, driving before him the Sere, Golo, Ndogo, and Bai until he reached Daim al-Zubair. Zemo captured hundreds of people and forced the rest to flee and take refuge among the Nyagulgule.[32] In 1890 Zemo launched a second attack and in the process besieged an allied force of Ndogo, Woro, and Nyagulgule at the stronghold

[31]N.R.O. Mahdiyyah 1/11B/7/162: Uthman Adam to the Khalifa, 28 April 1888.

[32]Santandrea, *Tribal History*, pp. 149-52.

of Sarago. After a long siege the Azande again forced the defenders to flee with heavy losses. Another Azande invasion the same year was launched by the powerful King Tumbura. From his base near the Congo-Nile divide, east of Zemo, he had extended his control northward to the river Boro. Upon the withdrawal of the Mahdists, he subjugated the Belanda, the Bongo, and other smaller groups around Wau.

By the 1890s the regions of the Bahr al-Ghazal and the Upper Nile had become part of the mainstream of the European scramble. King Leopold of the Congo initiated this competition in 1890 by sending an expedition to Equatoria. During the next three years several Belgian expeditions were sent to this region, the most important being the one led by Nilis in 1894. This expedition was sent to Hufrat al-Nahas, which Leopold believed to be a site of rich mineral wealth. The Kreish sultan of Hufrat al-Nahas, who happened to be at odds with the Mahdists, surrendered the mines to the Belgians. An agreement was signed in March 1894 stipulating that even if the influence of the Congo Free State ceased in these regions, the mines would pass in full right to Leopold and his heirs.[33]

The people of the western Bahr al-Ghazal were now compressed between the Belgians to the south and the Mahdists to the north. Their leaders sought to maintain their positions by shifting alliances between these powers. The Feroge, for instance, resisted the Mahdiya and fought Karamallah during his campaign in the area. The Nyagulgule, on the other hand, were the first to rise in support of the Mahdiyyah. After their defeat by the Azande, they placed themselves under the protection of the Feroge sultan. Thus, when they realized that they could not maintain their independence against two powerful forces such as the Azande and the Mahdiyyah, they made their peace with the Azande.[34]

---

[33]Robert O. Collins, *The Southern Sudan 1883-1898: A Struggle for Control* (New Haven: Yale University Press, 1964), p. 142.

[34]In September 1892, Hamad Musa and Hajar Dahiyyah wrote to Zemio requesting asylum in his land when they were threatened by the Ansar advance. N.R.O. Bahr al-Ghazal Province, 1/3/12, Notes on the Western District Tribes, 1927.

In 1893 the Bahr al-Ghazal was again threatened by the Mahdists who were increasingly concerned with the advance of the Congo Free State. Under the leadership of al-Khatim Musa, Mahdist forces invaded the territories of the Feroge. After a short engagement the Mahdists were forced to retire. Although victorious, the Feroge sultan Hamad Musa appealed to the Azande for support. By the beginning of 1894 both the Feroge and the Nyagulgule were in full retreat southward.[35]

The Mahdist presence prompted another Congolese advance. In March 1894, the Belgian resident in Zandeland began a march toward Raga, but he was soon recalled because of the critical situation in the upper Uele. He was replaced by Donckier de Doncel, who continued the advance to Raga. By July 1894, the Belgians had concluded a treaty with Hamad Musa of the Feroge, according to which Hamad would be the intermediary of the trade between the Congo Free State and all the area up to Darfur. This treaty was most significant for it not only opened up possibilities of trade for the Belgians in these regions but also secured for them a protectorate.[36]

In the meantime, al-Khatim had been assembling his forces at the end of the 1894 rainy season, and he now appealed to the local rulers to expel the Azande and the Congolese and to join him. Anticipating Congolese protection, the Feroge sultan rejected al-Khatim's appeal. However, the Belgians were totally unprepared to meet the Mahdist armies. They consequently retreated to Mojarne. This retreat convinced the Feroge of the futility of dealing with the Congolese, and the sultan therefore surrendered to al-Khatim.[37] Several other leaders who were angered by the

---

[35]Musa al-Mubarak al-Hasan, *Tarikh Darfur al-Siyasi, 1882-1898* (Khartoum: Khartoum University Press, 1964), pp. 214-18.

[36]Collins, *Southern Sudan*, p. 159.

[37]Among the captives was Ahmad Fartak, father of the late Isa' Fatak, the Feroge sultan during the colonial period. He was taken to Umdurman where he became a *mulazim* (companion) of the Khalifa until 1898. After the battle of Karari, in which he fought and was wounded, Ahmad Fartak fled with Ali Dinar to al-Fashir from which he

constant Congolese demands for supplies joined al-Khatim, and the Congolese were consequently forced to abandon their fort at Adda.

A final Congolese attempt against the Mahdists was halted by the vicissitudes of European diplomacy. In 1894, the Franco-Congolese Treaty was concluded, limiting the possessions of the Congo Free State in those regions. By February 1895, the Congolese had completely withdrawn from the Bahr al-Ghazal. The fate of the Mahdist expedition was no different. In 1895, an insurrection broke out in Darfur. Al-Khatim Musa was recalled to assist in quelling the rebellion and withdrew from the Bahr al-Ghazal, thus ending the Mahdist presence there.

The Mahdist occupation of the Bahr al-Ghazal was one of a long series of outsiders' attempts to control these regions. Like al-Zubair, Rabih, and Zemo, the Mahdists attempted to incorporate the area into their expanding domain, but their regime endured only a short time because their power was based on a precarious superiority of firearms and violence. However, they left behind a legacy of wars and conflicts that lasted until the end of the century. The Feroge began to expand, subjugating the Mangyat, the Kreish-Hufra, and the Binga, while Kara, Yulu, and several sections of the Kreish were engulfed in constant wars, raids and counter-raids that characterized the region's history.

By the end of the century, however, the history of Dar Fertit had entered a new phase and the contest over the control of the area was at its height. The struggle this time involved the French, who were advancing from the west, and the British who were approaching from Egypt up the Nile. Since the occupation of Egypt in 1882, Britain had become concerned with the security of the Nile waters upon which Egypt's life was entirely dependent. Britain was aware that no local power could present a threat. It was the other European powers, particularly the French who had similar ambitions, about whom the British worried. From their base in the Ubangi-Chari region the French began to advance east into the Bahr al-Ghazal through Dar Fertit. In June 1889 they

---

finally returned to Raga. N.R.O. Bahr al-Ghazal Province 1/3/12: Notes on the Western District Tribes, 1927.

arrived at Daim al-Zubair in an attempt to establish control over the area. The local rulers of the Feroge and the Nyagulgule were subdued without too much difficulty. At the end of the year an expedition was sent to Wau where a fort was built which came to be known as Fort Dessaix. Other posts were established at Tonj, Mvolo, and Chakchak.

The French attempt to include the upper Nile region in their domain was challenged by the British who were determined to ward off any other European power interested in the Nile. Thus following the Anglo-French confrontation at Fashoda and the French withdrawal, Britain established hegemony over the entire Nile basin. Indeed, the occupation of the Bahr al-Ghazal was a very crucial step in this direction.

Chapter 2

BRITISH CONQUEST AND THE ESTABLISHMENT OF THE COLONIAL ADMINISTRATION IN THE WESTERN BAHR AL-GHAZAL

The Anglo-Egyptian conquest of the Bahr al-Ghazal was a gradual process which began two years after the Fashoda incident. After a series of reconnaissances and battling with the formidable swamps, Colonel W.S. Sparkes Pasha, accompanied by the 14th Sudanese Battalion disembarked at Mashr'a al-Raqq on 12 December 1900.[1] After the establishment of a series of posts in the eastern and central parts of the province, Major W.A. Boulnois began his march to the west and the northwest in March 1901. He first advanced to Daim al-Zubair, whence he proceeded to Gossinga where he established a military post at the request of the local sultans, Nasir Andel and Musa Hamid.[2] Other posts were established at Chakchak, Busuiliya, and Daim Qinawi. Boulnois's mission was completed by Major D.C.E. Comyn who, in 1904-1905, had established Kafia Kingi, Raga, and Kabaluzu posts and

---

[1]The expedition consisted of five British officers, eleven Egyptian officers, and 266 irregular troops. These troops were dispatched from Umdurman on 29 November 1900 in two steamers. Amin el-Malouf, "The Occupation of Bahr al-Ghazal, Year 1901," *Journal of the Egyptian Society of Historical Studies* 2 (1952): 136-39.

[2]D.C.E. Comyn, *Service & Sport in the Sudan; a record of administration in the Anglo-Egyptian Sudan with some intervals of sport and travel* (London: John Lane, 1911), p. 139.

23

completed annexation of the historical "Dar Fertit" to the Condominium administration.

A number of factors facilitated this easy march of the invading forces. Emerging from the turmoils of the late nineteenth century, the fractionalized societies were not in a position to offer opposition to the newcomers. Moreover, from the outset the new regime was able to identify and conciliate a wide range of notables and local leaders. The expected benefits of cooperation also induced these leaders to accommodate the colonial regime. On 14 April 1900 a delegation arrived at Khartoum representing eleven *shiukh* and *salatin* from the province expressing their willingness to cooperate with the new government. The British impressed them with gifts, and confirmed them in their positions. They were sent back with flags and "robes of honor" for their leaders. Sultan Nasir Andel, Musa Hamid, Hussain Hamad, and Yambio were among those who received government presents.[3] They saw the colonial government as a purveyor of "peace and order."[4] When one understands the extent of destruction in the previous decades, it is easy to see how many people in the district eventually accepted colonial rule out of sheer moral and physical exhaustion.

The unique arrangement by which the Sudan was ruled affected the character and system of the administration in the newly conquered territory during the first two decades of Anglo-Egyptian rule. The terms of the Condominium Agreement, which was signed in January 1899, stipulated that the country would be ruled by Egyptian and British officials under the direction of a governor-general who was to be appointed by the khedive of Egypt but nominated by the British government. During the early days of colonial rule the administration was more-or-less direct all over the country and was military in nature. The chief object was simply the maintenance of law and order. The country was divided into primary administrative units called provinces, each under a British governor. The provinces were in turn sub-divided into districts under the supervision of British inspectors.

---

[3]Sudan Intelligence Report, no. 73, September 30, 1900, app. (b).

[4]Sudan Intelligence Report, no. 73, September 30, 1900, app. (b).

During the early decades of condominium rule the senior positions were filled from the ranks of British officers seconded to the Egyptian army. But gradually the balance shifted in favor of civilians who were recruited into a Sudan Political Service.[5] By the early 1920s the transition to civilian officials in the northern Sudan was virtually complete. In the South, however, this process was slower and military officers continued to form the backbone of the administrative staff. Since the government in Khartoum was very little involved in details of the administration in the South, those officers were left in almost complete control of affairs. But owing to the regime's financial difficulties, the chronic shortage of personnel, and local resistance, the British presence in the southern Sudan was very tenuous. During the first twenty years the administration was at best nominal with only a few posts, a handful of Egyptian and northern Sudanese troops, and even smaller number of British officials.

The immediate concern of the infant administration in the South was delineation of borders and establishment of an administrative machinery. From the government's perspective the division of people into easily recognizable ethnic entities was a prerequisite for any effective control. Accordingly the province was divided into six administrative districts: the Eastern, Central, Meridi, Yambio, Tembura, and Western Districts.[6] The districts were further subdivided into twelve administrative units called *mamuriyat*. Wau became the capital of the province where the governor and senior inspector resided. A British officer was stationed at the headquarters of each district, assisted by an a mamur.

According to the new administrative divisions, the historical "Dar Fertit" became the Western District of the Bahr al-Ghazal province. It was bounded on the north by the Bahr al-Arab, on the south and west by the Congo-Nile watershed, and on the east

---

[5]Robert O. Collins, "Sudan Political Service: A portrait of the Imperialists," *African Affairs* 71 (1972): 295.

[6]*Bahr al-Ghazal Handbook*, Sudan Government Publication, 1911, pp. 37-46.

by a line drawn north-south halfway between the Kuru and Sopo rivers. This was a vast region with an area of 36,000 square miles but a population estimated in 1930 at approximately 32,000 people, less than one person per square mile.[7] When Comyn was posted as inspector to Daim al-Zubair in 1904, he was the only British official in the district. He was assisted by one or two Egyptian mamurs and a small police force of which eighty men were posted at Raga, twenty-four at Daim al-Zubair, twenty-four at Kafia Kingi, four at Kabaluzu, and four at Gossinga.[8] British officials rarely visited most of the province and certainly several parts of the Western District never even saw a British administrator for ten years at a time.[9]

The peculiar characteristics of the Western District presented different kinds of problems to the British administration and hence conditioned its policies and strategies in the area. This was one of the most impoverished areas of the South; it was an arena of intensive cultural interaction, as reflected in the composition of its population; Islam predominated among the ruling families and the use of the Arabic language was widespread. The difference between the Western District and the rest of the province was depicted by a British official who stated that "it was obviously impossible to try a Mohammedan of Raga under the same conditions as a Dinka."[10] Thus, the Western District was administered almost along northern lines. Comyn and his successor, H. Walsh, saw administrative advantages in maintaining the pre-existing

---

[7]At first the district's headquarters were established in 1903 at Diam al-Zubair, garrisoned by an Egyptian battalion. Another post was founded at Kafia Kingi. Then in 1904 the Egyptian battalion was moved to Wau and only a detachment of the Jihadiyah was left at Diam al-Zubair. In 1906 the headquarters were moved to Raga and a mamur was left in charge of Diam al-Zubair (*Bahr al-Ghazal Handbook*, pp. 37-46).

[8]Bahr al-Ghazal Handbook, pp. 37-46

[9]N.R.O. Intel. 2/26/214, Military Report on the Western District, 1911.

[10]*Bahr al-Ghazal Handbook*, p. 37.

system of traditional authority in which the salatin were at the top, followed by the wkala and the shiukh.

Unlike many other parts of the Bahr al-Ghazal province, where British administrators became preoccupied with the identification of traditional leaders, several groups in the Western District were organized under their own headmen. As mentioned in the previous chapter, authority among the various ethnic groups in this area was vested in the hands of certain dynasties who occupied power centers by virtue of their assumed descent and their control of important economic resources. Traditionally, the salatin claimed all the land in their territories and required their subjects to pay tribute in the form of tusks and grain. The government policy was to work through these local rulers by which means the inspector had only to deal with seven salatin and shiukh in the whole district. Those groups who had no traditional rulers were placed under the nearest sultan regardless of their ethnic background, with the result that these rulers came to control multi-ethnic political units. In Raga, Sultan Musa Hamad of the Feroge extended his authority over fifty shiukh and wkala representing different ethnic groups such as the Ndiri, Mangyat, Mandala, and some Kreish sections. In Gossinga, the most prominent rulers were Nasir Andel of the Nyagulgule and Said Bandas of the Kreish-Naka.[11] In Kafia Kingi in the northwestern parts of the district, Sultan Muhammad al-Sughair became responsible for the Kreish section at Hufrat al-Nahas as well as for a few Binga and Kara. Further south, the inhabitants of Daim al-Zubair came under three rulers, Musa Komondogo of the Kreish-Ndogo, Sultan Yango of the Banda, and Sultan Gabir of the small Zande diaspora in the region.[12]

---

[11]Said Bandas was an ex-slave who was installed as ruler by the Waidaian sultan over the Kreish-Naka before their movement to the Bahr al-Ghazal as a result of al-Sanusi's raids.

[12]When the Catholic Bishop Geyer visited the Western District early in 1905 he reported that the territories of Musa Hamid covered an area of approximately 9,600 square miles. His rule extended over 3,500 Feroge, Kreish and other sections. Franz Xaver Geyer, *Durch Sand, Sumpf, und Wald* (Freiburg im Breisgau: 1914), p. 231.

It was customary for the salatin choose the wkala from their own ethnic group and post them to outlying areas. They carried out the sultan's orders in the collection of tribute and the recruitment of carriers. The power of the salatin to collect dues, ivory, and honey was upheld by the colonial government. Significantly, certain rulers were endowed with additional powers to perform a limited range of government functions. Musa Hamad and Nasir Andel, for instance, were allowed to give sentences of up to one month's imprisonment. While British officials in many parts of the South had to contend with a shortage or absence of leadership, the Western District fulfilled that demand.[13] Nevertheless, the first two decades were characterized by the frequent deposition and dismissal of local rulers on grounds of resistance, defiance, and misuse of power.[14]

British Economic and Social Policies in the Western District

British rule in the Sudan, as more generally in other parts of the world, was to secure access to cheap raw materials and develop new markets for commodities manufactured in Britain. The riverine areas of the northern and central Sudan lent themselves most readily to a form of development that could meet these objectives. From the perspective of the colonial administration, the North seemed to offer the best potential for economic development. The main areas of cultivation were comparatively close to the administrative and commercial capital of the country. The South was an entirely different story. In the late nineteenth century, the Belgians, and to a lesser extent, the French, were buoyed up by the "myth" of the Bahr al-Ghazal and its vast

---

[13]N.R.O., Intel. 2/26/214: Military Report on the Western District, 1911.

[14]Musa Hamid of the Feroge, for instance, was dismissed in 1908 owing to his resistance to the government. Ibrahim Dardig of the Dango was imprisoned and exiled in the north as a result of his support of Murad Ibrahim and Andel Abdullahi in their revolt against the government in 1912.

mineral deposits. However, the British labored under no such illusions. To them the South was no more than a military garrison for the protection of the Nile waters. Economic conditions in the southern Sudan in 1898 afforded small ground for optimism. The intractability of its environment, the scattered population, and above all, the extended and costly communications, all discouraged the colonial regime from instituting any form of investment in the region. Another factor that has to be taken into consideration was the regime's acute shortage of funds, as the entire country was heavily dependent on an Egyptian subsidy. Egypt's annual contributions to the Sudan's budget totalled over E£5 million by 1913, when they ceased. Moreover, during the same period the Egyptian government lent the administration E£5.5 million, interest-free and without any terms of repayment. These funds were almost entirely spent in the North, particularly in the riverine regions. The South was simply excluded from most programs. Issues such as economic and social development remained outside the immediate concern of the colonial regime in the South.

From the condominium government's point of view, the economic problems of the South fell into two groups according to geographical factors. First, it wished to realize the potential of the most promising agricultural zone in the ironstone plateau in the southwest, especially the fertile stretch of Equatoria along the frontier with the Belgian Congo between Tembura and Yei, known as the "Green Belt."[15] But the attainment of this objective was complicated by problems arising in the second region: the flood plains of the White Nile and Bahr al-Ghazal with the sudd (swamp barrier) at its center which rendered the "Green Belt" inaccessible and its exports uneconomic. Here the objective was to improve transport both on land and by river, and to tap the pastoral resources of the Nilotic peoples, if only to meet the costs of their day-to-day administration.[16]

---

[15] John Tosh, "The Economy of the Southern Sudan under the British, 1898-1955," *Journal of Imperial and Commonwealth History* 9/2 (May 1981): 277.

[16] Tosh, "Economy of the Southern Sudan," p. 277.

The South's economic prospects were blighted from the outset by one of the bloodiest and most prolonged periods of pacification anywhere in Africa. Moreover, there was an antipathy on the part of British officials to material progress in the South. The "fragile integrity of the tribe" had to be protected against any potentially disruptive external influences such as the inflow of cash, urbanization, and education.

In the Bahr al-Ghazal there was little scope for commercial exploitation of rubber and timber. Of all the districts in the province the Western District was, perhaps, the most unremunerative. Comyn's building budget was E£200; for road construction he allotted E£20. Agricultural production could meet only the bare requirements of local consumption. The main staple products were sorghum, sesame, maize, manioc, and varieties of millet. Natural catastrophes such as the lack or over-abundance of rain had frequently upset the balance between subsistence and famine. Thus, agriculture had to be supplemented by fishing and hunting. The entire province and the Western District in particular became heavily dependent on supplies imported from the north.[17]

The only easily-exportable product of importance in the Bahr al-Ghazal was ivory and the government moved mercilessly to exploit it.[18] Ivory export increased from fifteen tons, worth E£7,925 in 1901 to seventy-six tons, worth E£51,320 in 1905. Most of the exported ivory went to French Equtorial Africa where traders and locals could exchange it for firearms or export it to Kurdufan and other northern markets. Ivory export could not sustain the region; it is not surprising, therefore, that the Bahr al-Ghazal province could not finance its administration and consistently operated on a deficit. Table 1 illustrates the situation.[19]

---

[17]In 1909 alone it was estimated that at least 171,168 pounds of sorghum were imported to the Western District from Khartoum.

[18]It was estimated that about 3,000 elephants were destroyed annually in the Bahr al-Ghazal province at the beginning of this century. N.R.O. Intel. 2/26/214, Military Report on the Western District, 1909.

[19]*Bahr al-Ghazal Handbook*, p. 63.

Table 1

BAHR AL-GHAZAL REVENUE AND EXPENDITURE
(in Egyptian pounds)

Year	Revenue	Expenditure
1902	2,518	11,573
1903	2,000	17,761
1904	6,000	16,987
1905	7,058	22,850
1906	8,226	24,647
1907	11,067	26,288
1908	11,500	26,929
1909	14,709	30,404
1910	15,941	30,289

The economic problems of the Western District were compounded by its terrain, poor communications, and lack of infrastructure. The three administrative centers were far from Wau, the capital of the province. Raga is 207 miles northwest of Wau, and Kafia Kingi is 137 miles further north. The roads which linked them were impassable for eight months (from May to December) of the year owing to the floods of the Pongo, the Biri, and the Sopo rivers. Travel was restricted to foot or boat, contributing further to the isolation of the area.

All that remained for the colonial administration was the collection or extortion of taxes, tribute, and labor in return for "security." Taxes were necessarily light. No direct tax was levied in the Bahr al-Ghazal until 1910 when the Muslim *ushur* was first collected in the Western District. In a pathetic attempt to monetize the economy, the local people were required to pay taxes in cash and each working adult or head of family became directly responsible for acquiring a certain amount of cash. But since the circulation of money was so limited in the district, forced labor and requisition of grain were often imposed in lieu of taxes.

British administrators found it difficult to recruit sufficient laborers with the qualities they wanted and at the price they were willing to pay. The early administrators in the Western District complained about the supposed idleness of the local people toward labor. But their failure to recruit unskilled laborers had nothing to do with the unfamiliarity of the locals with wage labor; rather the conditions, the type of work offered, and the rate of pay were major disincentives. The average daily wage for unskilled labor in the district was thirteen milliemes (E£0.013). The work available was porterage, military and police service, and road maintenance. The local people had always avoided porterage and evinced little interest in military service. However, the French *prestation* (a labor tax which compelled adults to work for a number of days) in French Equatorial Africa had prompted many people to migrate to the Sudan. They were welcomed by the British and became a major source of cheap labor.[20] Thus the majority of people in the Western District continued to live on a cashless basis and the area remained very peripheral to the colonial economy. The monetization of the economy could not have been accomplished without the creation of an extensive demand for cash and a complete transformation of the economy.

In the fields of education and social services, there was hardly any progress. Since education was left in the hands of Christian missions, no government school was opened in the Western District until the mid 1920s. Consequently education was restricted to the few *khalawi* (Quranic schools) at Kabaluzu, Kafia Kingi, Gossinga, and Raga. Instruction was conducted by local as well as West African fakis (religious teachers).

The first two decades of the twentieth century were ones of epidemiological and ecological disaster in the Western District. Indeed, malaria, dysentery, leprosy, and venereal diseases were not new. However, the most serious epidemic in this area was trypanosomiasis or sleeping sickness. Early in 1905, there were strong suspicions that the disease had invaded the southern Sudan from Uganda and French Equatorial Africa. In 1909, two cases were discovered in the Western District. Consequently, quarantine camps were established. All immigrants that year were settled in

---

[20]N.R.O. Intel. 2/26/214, Military Report on the Western District, 1909.

selected villages along the main roads. In 1916 a Sudanese force was sent across the frontier to assist the French in quelling an uprising; this force operated in an area heavily infected with sleeping sickness and many of the soldiers returned to the Sudan with the disease. In 1917 about 4000 refugees from the French territories were settled around Tembura in the southern part of the Bahr al-Ghazal province, creating what came to be known as the Tembura epidemic of 1918. In the Western District, between 1905 and 1925 some seventy-three cases were detected and segregated, all but two of which were of immigrants from the French Congo. The methods that the government used to fight the disease included creation of well cleared settlements where those infected could live and be treated; then the enforcement of the permanent settlement of the inhabitants into healthy areas; the construction of well kept roads; and finally the supply of staff necessary for regular inspection.[21] Although the disease was not completely eradicated, it was at least reduced to minor proportions. But the people of the Western District continued to experience occasional outbreaks of epidemics that resulted in a continuous decline in the population of this already sparsely populated area. In 1907, for instance, measles claimed over fifty lives in Raga alone.[22]

Slavery

It is a commonplace that one of the most cherished and oft-repeated reasons for the conquest of the Sudan was to abolish slavery. Owing to the past preeminence of "Dar Fertit" in supplying slaves to internal and external markets, suppression of slavery and the attitude of the colonial administration toward it are vitally important to the history of the region.

---

[21]H.C. Squires, *The Sudan Medical Service An Experiment in Social Medicine* (London: William Heinmann, 1958), pp. 23-25.

[22]N.R.O. Intel. 2/26/214, Military Report on the Western District, 1911.

It is important to point out that during the first two decades of this century the attitude of the colonial government toward the institution of slavery in the Sudan was generally lax. Preoccupied with reinforcing their own tenuous hold on the country, condominium officials were obliged to tolerate, if only temporarily, the existence of slavery.[23] From their perspective servitude was an integral part of Sudanese life. To sanction wholesale emancipation of slaves, therefore, would provoke a social backlash and jeopardize their position in the country.

Owing to shortage of personnel and funds, no specific antislavery measures were established in the Bahr al-Ghazal during the early days of the condominum. Instead the provincial authorities naively appealed to all tribal chiefs within a fifty mile radius of Wau to stop trading in slaves. These verbal warnings were bound to be ignored as the government had no means of enforcing them. The age-old slave raiding and smuggling continued, not least in the old slave-raiding zones of "Dar Fertit" and the adjacent territories of French Equatorial Africa and Wadai. Although there is no evidence of continued large-scale operations, intermittent smuggling of slaves and arms bartering persisted in these regions. Slaves were captured and then passed in transit via Kafia Kingi, Kabaluzu, and Raga to the markets of Darfur and Kurdufan.[24] Arms were smuggled from Tripoli and sold in these regions. In addition to the continuing raids of Muhammad al-Sanusi of Dar al-Kuti, and Sultan Jallab of the Yulu, several other elements were

---

[23]For more details on British policies and strategies in regard to the question of slavery, see Taj Mohammed Hargey, *The Suppression of Slavery in the Sudan, 1898-1939* (Ph.D. dissertation: Oxford University, 1981).

[24]In 1915, the inspector of the Western District reported that a caravan was captured near Kabaluzu including twenty-four slaves from Dar Sila. N.R.O. Intel. 5/1/1, E.W. Mande to the Governor, Bahr al-Ghazal Province, 5 April 1915. It should also be noted that most of the salatin and the shiyikh in the district had traditionally kept domestic slaves in their households.

involved in this twin traffic.[25] These included a few jallaba and Levantine traders and West African pilgrims. In 1907, the assistant director of the Slavery Repression Department was convinced that most towns in the Western District concealed captives destined for the northern markets.[26]

Despite the government's initial appeal to local rulers in the province, slave smuggling persisted. The government simply had no means of enforcing any anti-slavery measures, and no specific posts were established in the province to prevent this illicit trade. The western headquarters of the Slavery Repression Department, located at al-Ubayyid in Kurdufan province, tried to monitor the trade routes from the Bahr al-Ghazal, but the vastness of the territory and its proximity to international borders made this task impossible. The elimination of the thriving twin traffic required a great deal of coordination between British and French officials on both sides of the western frontier. The first significant attempt at anti-slavery suppression was the meeting of French officials from adjacent Ubangi-Chari and the provincial officers at Raga in 1910. Proposals for joint action included introduction of verifiable identification documents for "legitimate" traders and pilgrims travelling between Kafia Kingi and Ndele in French Equatorial Africa and the formation of several additional posts at Jabal Jali and elsewhere in Wadai on the French side of the frontier.[27] These measures significantly contributed to the decline in slave smuggling across the borders.

The main problem for British officials came from within. The frontier between Darfur and the Bahr al-Ghazal was infested by

---

[25]N.R.O. Intel. 2/13/112, Director of Intelligence to the Governor-General, 22 October 1910.

[26]Sudan Intelligence Reports, no. 235, February 1914.

[27]In 1910 French and British representatives met at N'Dele to discuss this issue. They came to the conclusion that slave trading was not carried out on any large scale and certainly not by pilgrims. However, the French agreed to issue identification passes to all pilgrims and these passes would be checked at Kafia Kingi by British officials. SAD 300/1, A note by the governor of the Bahr al-Ghazal, 14 September 1910.

the Bandala and the Baqqara freebooters who pillaged the West African pilgrims. Initially, the Fellata had used the traditional route that passed through Ali Dinar's territory. But owing to frequent attacks by the sultan's armed bands, pilgrims began to use the southern route on which they likewise found no safety. Moreover, the age-old slave smuggling between the Bahr al-Ghazal and Darfur was revived under Ali Dinar. With the defeat of the Mahdists by the Anglo-Egyptian forces in 1899 Ali Dinar, grandson of the former Darfur sultan, Muhammad al-Fadl, returned from exile in Umdurman, seized the capital al-Fashir and defeated the puppet Mahdist sultan Abu Kuada. The condominium government, faced with the formidable problem of administering a vast territory, was unwilling at that time to undertake the additional burden of ruling this distant province. Ali Dinar was, therefore, recognized as the ruler of Darfur as long as he was " obedient" to government authority and paid nominal tribute.

One of the immediate concerns of the new sultan was the definition of his borders. Although Ali Dinar directed his attention mainly to the northern and western frontiers, he also relentlessly tried to restore Darfur paramountcy over the southern peripheries. In June 1903 Ali Dinar was complaining that unknown officers, either French or English, had crossed his border into "Dar Fertit" and hoisted a flag at Hufrat al-Nahas. They were treating the shaikhs insolently, arresting them, imprisoning them, and then taking them away to unknown places.[28] When it was explained that the unknown officers were the governor of the Bahr al-Ghazal province, and a British officer, who was leading a large patrol through a hitherto unadministered part of the province, Ali Dinar still grumbled that the governor should be instructed not to interfere with his subjects, and to stay within his own boundaries.[29] This frontier region had many attractions for the Fur sultan. In addition to the copper mines of Hufrat al-Nahas, some of its Muslim inhabitants were loyal vassals to the ancient Fur sultanate. Despite the presence of a colonial government in the Western

---

[28]N.R.O. Intel. 7/1-5, Ali Dinar to Slatin, 28 June 1903.

[29]N.R.O. Intel. 1/1-5, Ali Dinar to Slatin, 19 August 1903.

District, Ali Dinar did not hesitate to invoke residual loyalties among former clients such as the Feroge, Binga, Kara, and Dango. He continued to interfere in local affairs, appointing or confirming local leaders. Last but not least for Ali Dinar, the animist population south of the Bahr al-Arab formed a conveniently accessible reservoir of slave recruits.

Immediately after his return from Umdurman, Ali Dinar proceeded to reorganize his armed forces along the traditional line of recruitment by replacing suspected elements with new slave recruits. Thus the political and domestic utilization of slaves was a feature of Ali Dinar's rule in Darfur. Apart from his servile bodyguard, the sultan surrounded himself with eunuchs and concubines. For almost two decades, the Darfur sultanate continued to acquire slaves for military, agrarian, and domestic purposes from the traditional reservoirs of Dar Sila, Dar Runga, Dar Kara, and "Dar Fertit." In addition to these sources, slaves were acquired via the nominally subordinate Baqqara of southern Darfur. The most powerful of these cattle nomads were the Rizaiqat, the Habbaniya, and the Ta'isha, who reguraly raided the Dinka and the people of the western Bahr al-Ghazal across the Bahr al-Arab. Failure to pay their annual tribute in the form of cattle, grain, and slaves would bring reprisals to the Baqqara.

In addition to Ali Dinar's claims over the southern hinterlands, the personal rivalries between him and Shaikh Musa Madibu of the Rizaiqat turned the Bahr al-Arab into a war zone. Ali Dinar's reprisals included the ravaging of the Baqqara territories and the punishment of Madibo's supporters. As a result the Bahr al-Ghazal became not only an operational base for the Fur sultan, but a refuge for destitute Rizaiqat. Following a big battle with Ali Dinar at Kubon in 1914, about three thousand Rizaiqat took refuge in Kafia Kingi and Raga.[30]

Ali Dinar's successful and extensive raids, culminating in the virtual annihilation of the Rizaiqat and his ability to gain the loyalty and support of some local leaders, demonstrated that his claims in "Dar Fertit" were not necessarily fantasies. Up until the conquest of Darfur in 1916 British officials had very little control

---

[30]N.R.O. Intel. 8/2/11, Bahr al-Ghazal Intelligence Report, May 1914.

over the affairs of the Western District. They could do little but send the sultan verbal warnings, and his trade in firearms and slaves continued to thrive. As long as the sultan forwarded his annual tribute and paid lip service to enforcement of anti-slavery measures, relations between al-Fashir and Khartoum remained cordial.

Relations between Ali Dinar and the Anglo-Egyptian government took a serious turn on the eve of the First World War, when the sultan began to challenge the colonial regime openly. Hostilities reached a peak in 1916, when the government finally decided to conquer Darfur. Ali Dinar was killed and Darfur was brought under condominium jurisdiction.

The primary concern of the government after the conquest of Darfur was to reconcile the inhabitants of the province, and only secondarily to engineer a gradual social transformation. In contrast to other parts of the country, Darfur lagged far behind in the transition to a society characterized by "free" contractual labour obligation. Hence, instead of taking actions that would hasten the demise of domestic servitude, the government decided to maintain the status quo and adopted a gradualist approach. One of the principal reasons for advocating such a cautious strategy was the risk of alienating the volatile Baqqara. Indeed, domestic servitude is an age-old institution among the Baqqara.

One of the main problems that the colonial government had to face in the Bahr al-Ghazal was rehabilitation of retrieved slaves. Fearing that these people would be reenslaved if they were returned to their homes, British officials decided to settle them in the province. In general, adult males were enlisted in the army and the police or took up other employment. Moreover, the missionary establishment provided shelter for young boys until they were adults. However, rehabilitation of freed young girls presented a problem for British authorities.[31] Apart from placing these, mostly Muslim girls with the few available suitable parents, the

---

[31]The children retrieved were mostly from the slave caravan attacked by the Habbaniyah on the Bahr al-Arab in April 1915. Only after some months did they eventually arrive at Raga. N.R.O. Intel. 2/43/366, R.M. Feilden to Assistant Director of Intelligence, 29 December 1915.

government decided to put them under the custody of the missions, a move that was opposed by local Muslim leaders who were unwilling to accept the presence of these girls in Christian institutions.[32] It was suggested that the children should be entrusted to the care of especially selected *shaikhat* or matrons to supervise them until they reached adulthood, or that they be sent to the northern provinces.[33] But, for political reasons, British officials in the province opposed the removal of girls from their native land.[34] As agreed earlier, the ultimate responsibility for the children's welfare until they become adults depended not the shaikhat but on the local officials. Aside from providing basic occupational training and education for the children, the government also provided funds for other expenses including food and clothes. After considerable arguments and counter-arguments, a rudimentary "Children's Home" was eventually established at Raga in early 1916. This home continued to provide shelter for emancipated male and female slaves until its closure in 1924. However, the practice of the colonial government of forced labor and mass conscription for the army, had damaged its credibility as well as anti-slavery measures.

Intermittent slave smuggling and kidnapping of children continued throughout the 1920s. Numerous runaway female slaves successfully appealed to the officials not to return them to Baqqara, who invariably claimed them as their legal spouses. In the early 1920s British officals prohibited the jallaba from marrying local women or hiring them as peronal servants. These measures were reinforced by the Closed District Ordinance of 1922, which gave British officials greater freedom of action in the Darfur-Bahr al-Ghazal border. Yet, in spite of all government legislation, colonial officials in Darfur and the Bahr al-Ghazal had doubts about effective eradication of slavery in these two provinces.

---

[32]N.R.O. B.G.P. 1/5/26, Willis to the Civil Secretary, 3 July 1915.

[33]N.R.O. Intel. 2/43/366, from Bonham Carter, legal secretary to Governor-General, 25 August 1915.

[34]N.R.O. Intel. 2/43/366, C.S. Northcote to R.M. Feilden, 10 September 1915.

Throughout the 1920s, domestic slavery existed in the Western District and southern Darfur. In 1926 it was reported that 183 slaves in Raga, 213 in Kafia Kingi, and 279 in Kabaluzu had formally applied for emancipation.[35]

One of the most unusual forms of servitude in the Bahr al-Arab region was best exemplified by the Mandala. "Mandala" is the name given to servile dependents of the Rizaiqat and the Habbaniya. They lived in independent colonies on both banks of the Bahr al-Arab. In Darfur they were known as "Mandala" and in the Bahr al-Ghazal as "Bandala," both terms referring to a particular kind of dance.[36] Their presence in the western Bahr al-Ghazal dates to the nineteenth century when a few groups of slaves had escaped from their Rizaiqat masters and sought refuge with the Feroge and the Nyagulgule. In the Bahr al-Ghazal the Bandala eked out a living by fishing and hunting and acquired a reputation as excellent elephant hunters. They were organized in semi-autonomous settlements under their own headmen who were controlled by the Feroge shaikhs. The Bandala paid half of their tusks to the Feroge sultan in return for protection and patronage. The Feroge could not demand any work from the Bandala, for the latter could always threaten to cross the river into Darfur. Using the same tactic against the Rizaiqat, the Bandala were able to maintain their autonomy.[37] On the other hand, the Feroge made arrangements with the Baqqara by which the latter agreed to

---

[35]N.R.O. Bahr al-Ghazal Province 1/5/26, Assistant District Commissioner, Kafia Kingi to District Commissioner Raga, 20 April 1926.

[36]The Bandala were mentioned by Nachtigal who stated that "The Bandala, slave tribe scattered over the southern part of the country [Wadai], have to deliver 4 mudd of honey per head." Gustav Nichtigal, *Sahara and Sudan, Wadai and Darfur*, vol. IV (Berkeley: University of California Press, 1971), p. 181. Also see G.K.C. Hebbert, "The Mandala of the Bahr el Ghazal," *Sudan Notes & Records* 8 (1925): 187-94. Also AP2, Box 3/113, School of Oriental and African studies, London University.

[37]N.R.O. B.G.P. 1/3/12, Notes on the Western District Tribes, 1927.

recapture and return runaway Bandala, while the Feroge promised to return any slave who might escape from the Rizaiqat.

As in many parts of Africa, manumission and freedom did not necessarily mean the end of economic and social dependence of ex-slaves. The former master often remained the patron and the guardian of his freed slaves. Despite living in autonomous colonies at some distance from the Baqqara, the Bandala continued to recognize their ties with their former masters. In fact the Bandala, in their own view and that of the Baqqara, have never attained full freedom. A modified if loose social and political connection has been maintained between the two groups up to the present time. In the Bahr al-Ghazal the Bandala were organized into small clans which correspond to those of their masters such as "Awlad Mahamid," "Awlad Balul" and so forth. The relationship involved continuing deference on the part of the ex-slaves. They were expected to pay homage to ex-masters on social occasions. The Bandala acted as guides to Baqqara hunting parties in the Bahr al-Ghazal, and even became notorious for kidnapping children for them; intelligence reports of the condominium government were filled with such incidents. In 1916, for instance, the Bandala raided a Dinka villiage, carried off four boys, and took refuge among the Rizaiqat. The inspector of the Western District could do nothing but appeal to Nasir Andel. The Nyagulgule sultan wrote back stating that the boys were under the custody of Musa Madibo and that he had no control over the affair. In 1917 the Bandala penetrated deep into the southern parts of the Western District and took about forty Golo women to Darfur.[38] The Bandala remained beyond government control and British officials had to rely on the traditional rulers of the Feroge and Nyagulgule to track down these evasive people.

The Mandala attained this peculiar status either by asking their masters for manumission or by running away and remaining in the bush until their masters sooner or latter accepted the fait accompli and granted them the ambiguous status of "Mandala"

---

[38]N.R.O. Intel. 8/2/11, Bahr al-Ghazal Intelligence Report, 20 May 1917. Also see Appendix A.

rather than *abid* or slave.[39] The subordination of the Mandala to their ex-masters was further cemented by intermarriage and concubinage with peculiar characteristics. Ex-masters who retained the obligation of guardianship were supposed to approve the marriages of their ex-slaves. A Bandala could not marry without the approval of his nominal owner, and all the children were considered property of the wife's master. The dowry was a slave's payment of a nominal sum of money for temporary union rather than a proper Muslim marriage. On a man's death his property goes not to his offspring, but to another slave of the same master. If the Bandala is killed his *diya* or blood money is normally paid to his ex-master.[40]

This was the extent of the connection between the Mandala who were living in the Bahr al-Ghazal and the Baqqara. But those who were living with their masters in Darfur were required to render additional services and tribute. This was the reason for the Bandala proclivity to go to the Bahr al-Ghazal. British officials did not fully comprehend the situation until much later. To them, the Bandala were a nuisance. The opportunity to deal with this issue finally occurred in 1930, with the announcement of a "Southern Policy."

Population Movement

The colonial boundaries between the western Bahr al-Ghazal and Darfur, the eastern Ubangi-Chari, and Wadai did not change the traditional pattern of population movement in these regions. The extension of linguistic and kinship networks across the political boundaries made it easy for people to move back and forth quite freely. The boundary between the French territories and the Bahr al-Ghazal was not actually delineated and the frontier was not agreed upon until the late 1920s.

---

[39]AP Box 3/13, From G.D. Lampen to Governor of Darfur, 18 April 1929.

[40]N.R.O. Bahr al-Ghazal Province 1/3/12, Notes on the Western District Tribes, 1927.

Migration to the Western District originated from different sources and was motivated by a variety of reasons. Immigrants came from Darfur, Kurdufan, northern Sudan, and from West Africa. However, the largest number of immigrants came from French Equatorial Africa. They came for three principal reasons: to escape the slave raiding of Sultan Muhammad al-Sanusi of Dar al-Kuti from the 1890s onwards;[41] to flee from the French system of taxation and labor recruitment; and to rejoin their own people from whom they had been separated during past turmoil.[42] British administration in the Sudan appeared to be less demanding than the French in terms of labor and taxation. In addition to these factors there was the historical eastward migration of West African traders, peddlers, and pilgrims. Many of them never completed their journey to Mecca and settled permanently in these regions. They traveled through the Bahr al-Ghazal to avoid the raids and robberies of the Baqqara. In 1908 it was reported that there were at least 400 to 600 West Africans in Kafia Kingi en route to Kurdufan.[43]

The question of the boundary between the Sudan and French Equatorial Africa was raised immediately after the Fashoda incident. During the treaty exchange between the British and the French governments in 1899, the French appeared to be willing to forego Dar Sila if they were compensated by the inclusion of Tumbura District in their jurisdiction. The issue remained unsettled until much later. While the French resented the migration of their people into the Sudan, the British appeared to be quite willing to accept them, especially in the sparsely populated Western District. Although the Sudan government "would do nothing to attract immigrants, it can not be held

---

[41]Dennis D. Cordell, "The Delicate Balance of Force and Flight: The End of Slavery in Eastern Ubangi-Shari," unpublished paper presented at the African Studies Annual Meeting, New Orleans, 1985.

[42]In 1912, for instance, a caravan of two thousand pilgrims arrived at Kafia Kingi from Ndele. See Sudan Intelligence Reports, July 1912 [referred to hereinafter as SIR].

[43]Sudan Intelligence Reports, no. 165, July 1908.

responsible for the return of those who choose to come of their own free will as the Sudan laws do not permit of surrendering immigrants who have not committed crime."[44] Implicit in this was the desire to avoid setting a precedent by returning valuable immigrant laborers. When a section of the Banda was attacked by the French in 1908 and their leader appealed to the British authorities in the Western District, the inspector gladly responded: "I sincerely hope he crossed, I require more labor."[45] These refugees helped to alleviate the deficiency in the Sudan labor force both in quantity and quality. The local rulers were described as "extremely averse" to supplying recruits for the army. Thus most of the recruits were drawn from Banda and Kreish immigrants. The former were described as "of finer physique and [as making] good soldiers."[46] The refugees were willing to offer their labor for food and shelter in lieu of payment.

Following the assassination of al-Sanusi by the French in 1911, some members of his family and his close lieutenants fled to Ouanda Jali where his son Abdallah Kamun proclaimed himself sultan. From this site which was located on the caravan route to Darfur, Bahr al-Ghazal, and southern Chad, Kamun tried to revive his father's commercial empire. Threatened by further French attacks, he appealed to the British authorities in the Sudan.[47] His request to immigrate to Sudan created a dilemma for the British as the "present situation is different and has making of political difficulty unless matters can be arranged on the basis of mutual

---

[44]N.R.O. Intel. 2/13/112, Stack to Governor-General, 22 October 1911.

[45]N.R.O. Intel. 2/13/112, Stack to Governor-General, 22 October 1911.

[46]N.R.O. Intel. 2/26/214, Military Report on the Western District, 1911.

[47]N.R.O. Intel. 2/13/112, Assistant Director of Intelligence to Civil Secretary, 12 May 1912.

agreement between London and Paris."[48] British officials regarded Kamun and his followers as political refugees fleeing from another European power. Consequently, the inspector of the Western District and the mamur of Kafia Kingi were instructed to maintain the status quo and prevent any further immigration from French Equatorial Africa pending negotiations with the French government.[49] It was finally decided that Kamun would be allowed to enter the Sudan, provided that he and his followers would be disarmed and settled where they could be watched by the government. Further, no guarantees would be given to him if the French wanted his extradition.[50] On 28 December 1912 the French occupied Jabal Jali. Consequently Kamun led his followers across the border and on 2 January 1913 he surrendered to the British authorities in the Western District. Latter on he settled in Buram in southern Darfur.

The immigrants from the French Congo were not only members of al-Sanusi's family, but also large sections of the Banda, Kreish, Aja, and Borno. Although the imigration of these people into the western Bahr al-Ghazal predated the coming of both the British and the French, the largest exodus took place after the fall of Ndele (capital of Dar al-Kuti) in anticipation of further French violence. Despite the fact that these fears subsided with time, the immigrants remained in the Sudan to avoid French policies of forced labor and heavy taxation.[51]

In 1913 France and Britain agreed to submit the dispute over the boundary to arbitration but this did not occur owing to

---

[48]N.R.O. Intel. 2/3/112, Assistant Director of Intelligence to the Governor-General, 13 March 1912.

[49]N.R.O. Intel. 2/3/112, Governor of Bahr al-Ghazal to Assistant Director of Intelligence, 7 April 1911.

[50]N.R.O. Intel. 2/13/112, Stack to the Governor of Bahr al-Ghazal, 7 December 1912.

[51]Faisal Abdel Rahman Ali Taha, "The Boundary Between the Sudan, Chad and the Central African Republic," *Sudan Notes and Records* 60 (1979): 4.

the outbreak of the First World War. However, in 1919 the two governments agreed to prevent the settlement in their respective territories of "unauthorized" immigrants, whether individuals or ethnic groups. But these resolutions remained on paper.

One of the most important moves from the French territories was that of Sultan Jallab and his Yulu subjects. Before the downfall of Dar al-Kuti, when al-Sanusi began to feel the threat of the increasing European presence in the region, he began to make plans to abandon his capital, Ndele, and move east. He sent one of his generals to prepare a move to Jabal Jali, which was the site of Sultan Jallab. Prior to that, relations between the two sultans were cordial and there was a great deal of trade in arms and ivory between them. However, relations began to deteriorate when Yulu bands began to attack al-Sanusi's caravans. According to local traditions, al-Sanusi despatched a delegation to Jallab, inquiring about his intentions. One general was killed and the rest were mistreated. Al-Sanusi regarded Jallab's action as an act of war. Consequently, an expedition was sent to punish Jallab and expel him from Jali.

The Yulu sultan was defeated and fled with a large number of followers to the mountains in the border region. Starvation and continued harassment by al-Sanusi's bands forced Jallab to flee to Kafia Kingi.[52] The Yulu sultan and his four hundred followers were ordered by British officials to move to Daim al-Zubair.[53] However, after the elimination of al-Sanusi, Jallab slipped off to the inaccessible mountains in the border region and began to send bands of followers to assist his brother-in-law Andel Abdullahi in his attacks against the Binga of Kafia Kingi. Jallab, however, was not quite comfortable in the French territories and feared that his fate would probalbly match al-Sanusi's. In 1922 he and his followers appeared again in Khandaq near Kafia Kingi. He was told to settle on the Boro River. A third of his followers remained at Khandaq but Jallab remained at large. The British then resorted

[52]Interview with Ibrahim Musa Ali, 25 July 1987.

[53]N.R.O. Intel. 2/13/112, Bahr al-Ghazal Intelligence Report, December 1912.

to the usual practice: the Yulu were divided and Ibrahim Kiyuku was set up as a rival to Jallab. However, following the reorganization of 1930, the two Yulu sections were reunited under Jallab and settled along the government roads.

The boundary question was finally settled in the 1924 Protocol between the British and French authorities. To enable the detached tribes to reach the main bodies of their people, the protocol permitted natives on either side of the frontier a period of six months during which they were to choose the territory in which they wished to reside permanently. On the expiry of this period, unauthorized movement of groups or individuals was to cease.[54] The majority of refugees were settled along the road between Daim al-Zubair and Raga, a short distance from the border. These settlements continued to attract immigrants from the Central African Republic as late as the 1920s. British authorities remained very ambivalent towards immigration from French Equatorial Africa, and it was only after the outbreak of sleeping sickness that certain measures to control it were taken.

Resistance and Rebellion in the Western District

The first two decades of the twentieth century have some unity in southern Sudanese history. It was a period of raw and brutal intrusion by the developing colonial state into the lives of Southern people. Numerous expeditions were sent through the forests and hills to bring defiant leaders to heel. In the western Bahr al-Ghazal the provision of peace and order and the confirmation of the ruling elites in their traditional positions were the primary reasons behind their initial accommodation to British rule. However, this situation was short-lived and soon turned into rebellions and uprisings. These were linked not only to the way in which colonial rule was imposed but also to the way in which it was subsequently conducted.

Resistance to the colonial regime was motivated by several factors and took various forms ranging from military confrontation to migration and to other forms of disobedience. For the most

---

[54]Taha, "The Boundary," p. 10.

47

part rebellions were rather local and seldom involved more than one village or ethnic group. Another feature of the Western District's resistance was the large-scale use of firearms. The reason is obvious: the local people were exposed to the use of firearms from the nineteenth century and many people mastered the art of manufacturing them. Moreover, there was a great deal of trafficking in firearms in these regions. Hence, while other southern societies relied on traditional weapons, the people of the western Bahr al-Ghazal confronted colonial forces with guns.

The matters around which scattered uprisings revolved were manifold. The government's intervention in local affairs such as the administration of justice and the settlement of local disputes, had undermined the position of ruling elites who tried to maintain their power and the independence of their political institutions. Another contributing factor was the frequent deposition of leaders. The presence of Mahdist elements in the Western District was another source of hostility towards the colonial government. Following the Mahdist defeat in 1898, large numbers of ex-Mahdists from the Feroge, Nyagulgule, and the Kreish returned to their homes and became a ready reserve for rebels. The West Africans played a major role in propgating the Mahdist cause. This Muslim dimension was indeed a unique feature of the Western District's resistance. Last but not least was the role of Ali Dinar who continuously enticed local leaders to rise up against the British.

The first leader to oppose the government was Musa Hamid of the Feroge. Musa felt threatened by transfer of the district's headquarters from Daim al-Zubair to Raga, the seat of Feroge rule. He made several attempts to move with his people and join Muhammad al-Sanusi in Ndele. British officials disliked him: he was described as a "very autocratic ruler and heavy drinker."[55] In 1907 he was suspected by Sudan Government officials of murdering a government soldier in Raga. Consequently he fled to French Equatorial Africa. As soon as he reached there he was arrested by French authorities and handed over to the British. Subse-

---

[55]N.R.O. Bahr al-Ghazal Province 1/3/12, Notes on the Western District Tribes, 1927.

quently he was exiled to Sinnar on the Blue Nile and later to Khartoum where he stayed for six months. He was released in 1908 and returned to the Western District whence he fled again to the French territories. Musa was finally deposed in absentia, and replaced by Ahmad Fartak.[56]

The next rebels after Musa were Murad Ibrahim and Andel Abdullahi of the Kreish. Their revolt, unlike that of Musa Hamid, was violent. Murad was deposed in 1908 as a result of a dispute between him and the inspector, and he subsequently fled to Ubangi-Chari where he was later joined by Andel Abdullahi of the Binga. The latter had been impressed by the French since their arrival in the region in the late nineteenth century, when they had given him presents.[57] In 1903 he was arrested by the British and sent to Wau as an outlaw. En route he slipped off and joined Murad Ibrahim in French territory to organize resistance against the British. Having organized their men, the two leaders marched against government forces at Hufrat al-Nahas and Kafia Kingi. After an inconclusive attack, they retreated to Sultan al-Sanusi at Ndele. As they were preparing to strike again, their plan was foiled by the French assassination of al-Sanusi in 1911. Thus the French occupation of Ndele forced them to flee to the Sudan. Mustering three hundred rifles, Andel sought out and shot those locals who had co-operated with the government. This action alienated many people and led to the failure of his revolt. Finally he and Murad Ibrahim invaded Kafia Kingi in 1912 to attack the Binga with whom Murad had long-standing hostility and to crush the government forces there. But this time they were overwhelmed by government troops and badly defeated.[58]

By the 1920s large-scale resistance in the Western District had finally subsided. Nevertheless, violent incidents and military confrontation between colonial officials and local people continued.

---

[56]N.R.O. Bahr al-Ghazal Province 1/3/12, Notes on the Western District Tribes, 1927.

[57]Comyn, *Service and Sports*, pp. 222-23.

[58]N.R.O. Intel. 2/13/113, Inspector, Western District to the Governor, Bahr al-Ghazal Province, 3 December 1912.

In April 1915, Shaikh Adam Abdullahi of the Binga informed the mamur of Kafia Kingi about an outbreak of cerebral meningitis among his people. The mamur went to the villiage accompanied by twenty police men. As a preventive measure the mamur burned about 150 huts. His mistake was that he did not explain his action to the hostile Binga. As a result, on their way back the mamur was attacked by a gang of angry Binga. After an exchange of gun fire, in which at least 853 rounds of ammunition were fired, two policemen were killed and the Binga lost thirteen men.[59] Violence remained an integral part of life in the Western District. Peace and security hardly existed beyond government posts.

---

[59]N.R.O. Intel. 8/2/11, Bahr al-Ghazal Intelligence Report, 1915.

Chapter 3

CHANGING PERSPECTIVES

Initially, after the conquest, the British administration in the Sudan was direct and had a military character. Individual officers, with enormous discretionary powers, were stationed in various parts of the country. The chief object of the administration was maintenance of law and order. However, the colonial authorities were quick to realize the shortcomings of a direct administration in such a vast country and with few British personnel. Moreover, following the mutiny of the Sudanese units of the Egyptian army in 1924, the administration could not rely upon Egyptian officers. An equally serious factor was the appearance in 1919-1924 of a national feeling among the educated class. Hence the decade of the 1920s marked the beginning of a new administrative strategy in the Sudan. This policy is generally known as "indirect rule" and is particularly associated with Lord Lugard and northern Nigeria.

As the British conceived it, indirect rule was a system through which traditional rulers were regarded as an integral part of the machinery of government. Its essence was that the colonial government should refrain from interference in the details of administration and allow a native agency to perform these simple functions. This meant the recognition, or the creation of chiefs whose primary function was to collect taxes and to preserve administrative control. Moreover, indirect rule was regarded as a device that would obviate the need for a large bureaucracy and thereby reduce the cost of administration. The theory of native administration also subsumed a set of views, images, and perceptions held by colonial officials about African societies and cultures. Central was the presumption that there existed an integrated body politic, reciprocal rights, and obligations between African rulers and their subjects. African societies were perceived as a mosaic of "tribes," each immutably living in its own ambience. Tribalism and ethnicity were therefore emphasized and became the cornerstone of the principal of native administration and a theoretical prerequisite for its application.

The system of native administration was far more successful in the northern Sudan where a centralized system of authority was far more developed and traditional chiefs were readily available. The existence of a common language and religion in the North was also a contributing factor to the application of the new policy in that part of the country. Conditions in the South, however, were different. The first two decades of colonial rule in the region were a period of neglect, punctuated by local resistance and official violence. Between the years 1910 and 1920 there were major revolts among the central and eastern Nuer as well as the Aliab Dinka. These were not mere scattered and isolated incidents but large scale rebellions that transcended ethnic boundaries. The government responded by sending punitive expeditions so powerful and destructive that they were operations of war rather than expedients of native administration. In order to bring these rebellious groups to heel, the colonial forces adopted a scorched earth policy, expropriating cattle, destroying crops, and burning houses. The magnitude of these operations reduced British presence in the South to that of a military garrison rather than a government. However, by the First World War colonial expeditions had generally accomplished their goals, although local resistance had not completely subsided.

Another factor that militated against the application of indirect rule in the South was the region's past experience. The activities of the slave traders and the Mahdist invasions that followed had contributed in different ways to disruption of the traditional socio-political structure of southern people. Thus, indirect rule in the South never progressed beyond the stage of judicial devolution. Judicial devolution meant the creation of a uniform network of courts known as "chiefs courts" whose purpose was to "relieve the district commissioner of the countless number of petty litigations and to teach the chiefs and their people that the former are responsible for their country and that the latter must look to their chiefs in the first instance."[1] It was assumed that administrative functions would evolve from the judicial process. Consequently, the courts were granted authority to perform a wide range of administrative duties. They were first instituted in Mongalla province in 1922 and by the middle of the 1920s had multiplied rapidly in different parts of the South. By 1925 all the districts of the Bahr al-Ghazal had courts.

In general, progress in judicial devolution was rapid and effective among the Azande and the Shilluk who possessed a highly centralized political authority as well as an institutionalized leadership. Among some Nilotic societies, political systems were fragmentary and leadership was widely dispersed; the government could not find a political hierarchy onto which it could easily graft the system of native administration. Judicial devolution among the Nilotes was therefore very slow.

In the western Bahr al-Ghazal, however, it is not hard to find centralized authority among groups such as the Feroge, Nyagulgule, Kreish, Yulu, Binga, Kara, and Banda. These units were ruled by a number of salatin and shiukh. The pattern of ethnic configuration and nature of these political units defied the colonial concept of ethnicity and tribalism upon which indirect rule was based. The pattern of political organization was one of shifiting relations between migrant groups of rulers and a variable number of followers. Ruling families occupied power centers by virtue of their control of important resources, their role in long-distance trade, and their claim of "superior" descent. These power centers attracted followers who sought access to these resources and protection against external attacks.

The ruling family of the Feroge claimed that they originated from a Borno pilgrim who, in one version, was called Hamad Abbas Himyar (implying a South Arabian origin). He was nick-named Feroge (from Arabic *farraq*, meaning separate), when he departed from his group. He married the daughter of the local chief of the Kaligi who lived at that time around Jabal Tambili north of Raga. The Kaligi became Muslims and adopted the name

---

[1]N.R.O. B.G.P. 1/5/1, Governor of Bahr al-Ghazal to the Civil Secretary, 26 October 1927.

Feroge, while Hamad's son Hasan set about creating a small polity. Hasan's authority was recognized by the Fur sultan Muhammad al-Husain who granted him a set of drums, the symbol of separate but subordinate authority within the Fur sultanate.[2] Organized after the fashion of their Fur lords, the Feroge began to move south, conquering several groups such as the Indiri, Togoyo, Mangayat, Shaiu. Thus the Feroge polity incorporated people of diverse ethnic backgrounds. The term Feroge, which was originally confined to the ruling family, was applied to their subjects. The sultan appointed several shiukh and wkala who became responsible for collection of tribute and other dues. Thus the relationship between the Feroge and their subject tribes was based on a loose political alliance which involved payment of tribute in return for protection. According to the 1927 tax list the Feroge subjects comprised the following: 38 members of the ruling family; 266 Bandala; 7 Kreish; 153 Shatt; 110 Nyagulgule; and 82 slaves.

Similarly, the Nyagulgule comprised several groups. The ruling family claimed a Bego origin. Two or three centuries ago, they migrated to Jabal Telgona and, with the help of Darfur, imposed themselves on the local people such as Nyagulgule, Tobago, and some Kreish sections. However, unlike the Feroge, the term Nyagulgule referred to the indigenous group and was later applied to the ruling family.[3] The process of fusion and fission was also vivid among the Kreish. The term Kreish was applied by outsiders to several groups of people who spoke similar languages. As mentioned earlier, they were divided into three clans: Kreish-Naka, Kreish-Hufea, and Kreish-Ndogo. The same can be said about the Aja, Binga, and Kara. Hence, the authority of the local rulers was more or less territorial. It was common habitat, occupation, and political association that created the bonds out of which centralized authority emerged. These groups were not discrete entities but open communities. They became

---

[2]Santandrea, *Tribal History*, pp. 141-44; Dennis Cordell, "The Savanna Belt of North-Central Africa" in *History of Central Africa*, vol. 1, ed. David Birmingham and Phyllis Martin (London: 1983), pp. 30-74.

[3]N.R.O. Bahr al-Ghazal Province 1/3/12, Notes on the Western District Tribes, 1927.

interdependent and integrated by the facts of settlement, subordination, and resistance to external pressures. This fluid ethnic situation frustrated the effective application of indirect rule which emphasized the existence of clearly defined "tribal" units. The efforts of British officials to arrange these people along ethnic lines proved futile.

Courts in the Western District varied widely in their composition, powers, procedures, and in the customary law which they applied. In some parts of the district Islam became the basis for the administration of justice, particularly among the Feroge, Nyagulgule, and other Muslim groups.

One of the major problems of the chiefs' courts in the western Bahr al-Ghazal was the lack of a common language in which the proceedings could be recorded. A pidgin Arabic was widely spoken in this part of the South. However, for several reasons that will be discussed later, Arabic was discouraged in the South. The first serious attempt to resolve the language question in the South as a whole was made in 1928 when the Rejaf Conference was held. The conference was supposed to recommend group languages for different parts of the South. Accordingly Zande was recommended as a group language in the Western District. However, Zande was spoken by very few people in this area and the only government school in the district was using Ndogo as a language of instruction. The missions and colonial authorities could not agree on this issue until the 1930s during the reorganization of the Western District. However, proceedings of Muslim courts continued to be recorded in Arabic. It was impossible, therefore, to establish uniform regulations or an ordinance that could be universally applied in the district.

The chiefs' courts and the administration in the Western District were reorganized after the general population reshuffle in 1930. As a result, the successful functioning of the chiefs' courts and the whole system of native administration during this era became dependent upon British officials. Chiefs were selected for their subservience and frequently removed when they failed to serve their purpose. Indirect rule in the western Bahr al-Ghazal as in many other parts of the South remained a spurious doctrine and the essence of the adminstration did not change: it continued to be as direct as ever.

55

Perhaps the only noticeable change during the 1920s was the substitution of civilian administrators for military officers who prevailed in the South during the first twenty years of British rule. Unlike their colleagues in the North, colonial officials in the South were seconded from the army and retained their army ranks. They joined the civil service on a contract basis. In this respect inspectors and mamurs were replaced by district commissioners who made their administrative headquarters in the districts themselves instead of in the province capitals. In the North, following removal of the Egyptian personnel after the 1924 incidents the school for training Sudanese substitutes was closed. Nevertheless, the few Sudanese officials produced were stationed mainly in the North in line with Southern Policy. The pattern of administration that prevailed during the first two decades persisted well into the 1920s. British district commissioners continued to be the main authorities in their districts. As their number increased, local mamurs were reduced and strictly limited to subordinate roles until they were finally removed in the late 1920s.

However, this generation of British administrators tended to stay longer than their predecessors, the inspectors and the mamurs. In the Western District, they were best exemplified by G.K. Hebbert and J. Macphail. Macphail was posted to the Western District at the end of 1925 after serving three years in the North. He was first stationed at Kafia Kingi while Hebbert was stationed at Raga. Hebbert was then transferred in May 1928 leaving Macphail, who had just moved to Raga, to be in charge of the district. Moreover, British officials were encouraged to learn local languages and carry out ethnographic research. Social science of the period, largely under the rubric of anthropology, was directed to identify "tribal" units and tribal chiefs. By the mid twenties a great deal of information on the histories and languages of the different groups in Western District had been compiled. These studies provided some initial clues about the histories and social organization of these societies. At the same time they served as a guide for sorting out, rearranging, and relocating the multifarious and fragmented groups in the district. On the basis of the most slender information, British officials decided who belonged to the Western District and who did not. Accordingly province administrators targeted two groups: the Shatt and the Dombo.

The Shatt were a branch of the Nilotic Luo called the Thuri. During the course of the Luo migration the Shatt followed the Bahr al-Arab toward the west, where they scattered in the border region between the Bahr al-Ghazal and Darfur. The majority of them, however, settled among the Dinka in the Bahr al-Ghazal. The Shatt identify themselves as Nilotes and their language is similar to the Shilluk language.[4] They were assimilated to such an extent that they became totally indistinguishable from the Shilluk.

Following the administrative division of the Bahr al-Ghazal province at the beginning of this century the Shatt were split between the Northern and Western Districts. The bulk of the group came under the jurisdiction of the Northern District where they lived independently on fishing and hunting. Moving back and forth between these territories, the Shatt never came under any government control or paid taxes. Shatt independence was anathema to colonial authorities who simply regarded these people as "outlaws." The Shatt had to be fixed in one place where they could be taxed and provide the labor needed for building government roads and rest houses. British officials firmly believed that the Shatt's original home was the Western District and that therefore they should be settled there. At the same time the small Dombo settlements in the Western District should be moved to the Northern District.[5] The Shatt settlement among the Dinka provided a sanctuary for those living in the Western District. A Shatt from the Western District could easily pass as a Shilluk or Dinka and enter the Northern District without difficulty. In this way they managed to evade government control. Consequently it was decided that all the Shatt should be moved from Northern District to the Western District. In addition to administrative convenience there were other motives behind the relocation of the Shatt. Prominent among these was the need to increase the number of

---

[4]Stefano Santandrea, *The Luo of the Bahr al-Ghazal* (Bologna: Editrice Nigrizia, 1968), pp. 59-61.

[5]N.R.O. Bahr al-Ghazal Province 1/5/301, Wheatly to D.C.s Western and Northern Districts, 12 October 1926.

people in the sparsely populated Western District, thereby creating an additional source of cheap labor.

The Shatt movement proved to be a difficult task. In the first place, the Northern District's Shatt were fully integrated into the Dinka society. They were not ready to abandon their pastoral way of life and move to the Western District which was infected with the tsetse fly. Moreover, their Nilotic kinsmen were willing to protect them and on several occasions the Dinka prevented the Western District's police from capturing the Shatt.[6]

The Shatt movement became a subject of heated debate and a source of friction between Hebbert and Owen, assistant district commissioner Northern District. In Hebbert's view, the Shatt movement would not be accomplished without pressure from the Northern District. But Owen had neither the will nor the time to "go Shatt hunting."[7] Wheatley, the province governor, was furious and said to Owen: "your letter to the D.C. Western District is a great disappointment to me, it shows the most regrettable lack of the spirit of cooperation which is essential if the administration is to be run efficiently and without friction."[8] Yet despite a rambling and voluminous correspondence, the matter remained unresolved. The Shatt riddle was inherited by successive British officials in the province in the late 1920s.

In 1929 a series of meetings was held between Macphail and Taylor who had succeeded Owen as district commissioner, Northern District. It was decided that the Shatt would be settled in Gall, four miles from the Northern District boundary. At the same time the Dinka were allowed to graze in certain parts of the

---

[6]One of these encounters took place in 1927 when a small band of armed Dinka were able to release fifteen Shatt after they had been captured by the Western District police. N.R.O. Bahr al-Ghazal Province 1/5/30, Hebbert to Owen, 15 June 1927.

[7]N.R.O. Bahr al-Ghazal Province 1/5/30, Owen to Hebbert, 10 August 1927.

[8]N.R.O. Bahr al-Ghazal Province 1/5/30, Wheately to Owen, 22 October 1927.

Western District.[9] A few months later Macphail wrote to Taylor about his dilemma, "As far as I am concerned we are no nearer a solution of the question than we were two years ago. I can not make my new poll tax lists as a lot of these people on my list are in your district, and still do not know whether they are Shatt or Shilluk. You say they are Shilluk. My chiefs say they are Shatt."[10] After reviewing the subject Brock, the new governor, decided to stick to his predecessor's decision; all the Shatt should be settled in the Western District and all the Dombo and the few Shilluk should go to the Northern District.[11] It was also decided that the boundary between the two districts should be moved to the Sopo River.

The Shatt "problem" lingered well into the thirties during which the Western District witnessed the greatest population reshuffle. The Shatt were ordered to move to the Kuru River. A few clans moved but the majority remained in the Northern District. Later British officials realized that this move was a "mistake" and that the Shatt were "quite different from other Western District tribes." It was finally decided that the Shatt should be given the choice between the two districts. Anyone found outside his district of "adoption" would be imprisoned. Yet these official decisions did not mean anything to the Shatt who continue to move freely to this day. Neither the colonial nor the post-colonial governments in the Sudan were able to bring them under control. The whole matter revealed the sort of issues which preoccupied colonial officials. Government efforts to organize people into easily recognizable ethnic entities were wrecked by the fluid ethnic situation in the western Bahr al-Ghazal. The extension of kinship ties accross boundaries made it easier for people to disregard administrative boundaries and move freely.

---

[9]N.R.O. Bahr al-Ghazal Province 1/5/30, Macphail to Brock, 31 January 1929.

[10]N.R.O. Bahr al-Ghazal Province 1/5/30, Macphail to Taylor, 6 March 1929.

[11]N.R.O. Bahr al-Ghazal Province 1/5/30, Brock to D.C.s Western and Northern Districts, 25 May 1929.

In 1929, S.R. Simpson arrived in the Western Distirict as assistant district commissioner. Upon his arrival he wrote to his fiancee: "The Bahr al-Ghazal or the Bog—as it is more commonly known—is forgotton in Khartoum, and the Western District is forgotton in the Bog."[12] The province budget showed a deficit of E£32,000. It seemed, wrote Simpson later, "that the economic blizzard, which a year or so later was to cause sweeping cuts in government expenditure (including a reduction in our pay) had already reached the Western District."[13] Raga and Kafia Kingi were steadily decreasing in prosperity. All the able-bodied in the district were supposed to pay the poll tax at the rate of twenty-five piastres. But there was no market for their grain and no other resources except beeswax and honey. Twenty-five piasters, therefore, was difficult to raise. Simpson's staff consisted of a mamur, an accountant-cashier, a clerk, a Syrian medical officer, and a police force of eighty men in Raga and thirty-five in Kafia Kingi. Simpson also questioned the wisdom of organizing the chiefs' courts along ethnic lines: " tribes are too numerous and too widely scattered to make any scheme of purely tribal courts feasible."[14] In his view, these courts should be organized on a territorial not a tribal basis. His rule became one of the landmarks in the history of the Western District. It was during his term that the district witnessed one of the most drastic changes in its recent history: the application of the Southern Policy.

By the early twenties, criticism of government policies in the Southern provinces was mounting. The regime's failures were avowed by a number of senior officials and manifested in the slow progress in native administration, and an appalling economic underdevlopment. The colonial administration imputed these failures to the erosion of "traditional cultures" in the South by "alien" influence represented by the facade of Muslim and Arabic traits which existed in some parts of the South. From the perspective of colonial administrators, these influences had

---

[12]SAD 720/4, Simpson Papers.

[13]SAD 720/4, Simpson Papers.

[14]SAD 720/4, Simpson Papers.

60

disrupted the "tribal" system and hindered implementation of indirect rule. Hence, Islam should be debarred in the South. British officials in Khartoum and in the South became convinced that there was need for a more comprehensive administrative program for the region. This program was elaborated by Sir John Maffey, the governor general, in 1928-1929 and was approved by the Foreign Office toward the end of 1929. It was announced by MacMichael in his famous circular of 25 January 1930. The essence of the so-called Southern Policy was expressed in the much-quoted paragraph of MacMichael's memorandum:

> The aim of the government policy is to build up a series of self-contained racial and tribal units with structure and organisation based, to whatever extent the requirements of equity and good government permit, upon indigenous customs, traditional usage and beliefs.[15]

This was the philsophy behind the Southern Policy which became a major theme in the repertory of Sudanese politics. Southern Policy has been sufficiently addressed in numerous works in a manner that warrants no recapitulation. What should be emphasized here is that MacMichael's memorandum was little more than an explicit statement by the civil secretary of policies that had been pursued in the South for at least two decades. Several British administrators during the first twenty years of this century shared the view that there would be no progress in the South unless the region was separated from Khartoum and granted some form of administrative autonomy. The great distance between the region and the capital as well as the poor system of communications were considered major obstacles to administration. Ideas such as the separation of these provinces, or their attachment to some East or Central African colonies, were contemplated by representatives of the Milner Mission, as well as by several

---

[15]N.R.O. Bahr al-Ghazal Province 1/1/1, MacMichael to Southern Governors, 25 January 1930.

Southern administrators themselves, but never seriously considered in Khartoum.[16]

Ideological and political considerations also played their part in the propagation of Southern Policy and the curtailment of Islamic influence in the South. Northern Sudan was in the British view part of the "Muslim East" and an extension of a "stagnating" Arab culture.[17]

British images of the northern Sudan were further shaped by their experience with the Mahdi and the assassination of General Gordon, the archetypal Victorian Christian gentleman. The threat of a militant Mahdist uprising continued to be a nightmare and a major preoccupation of British officials during the early phases of their rule in the Sudan. To allow the spread of Islam in the South would be

> to sprinkle gun powder in the neighborhood of a powder Magazine . . . the resultant danger, too, is double-edged; for not only would the Arabs in the event of a rising, be able to call upon the South in the name of a common religion, for instance, but, if there were trouble between the government and the negroes in the South, these same Arabs of the North and the intelligentsia of the towns would not fail to assume a pose of sympathy and interest which might become a serious embarrassment.[18]

In brief, Islam was seen as a dangerous political weapon not only in the Sudan but also in other parts of Africa. The southern Sudan should, therefore, remain "uncontaminated."

---

[16]They included Chauncey Hugh Stigand, Governor of the Upper Nile Province from 1917 to 1918, and Woodland, Governor of Mongalla Province from 1920 to 1924.

[17]Robert O. Collins, *Shadows in the Grass: Britain in the Southern Sudan, 1918-1956* (New Haven: Yale University Press, 1983), pp. 172-73.

[18]F.O. 371/13865, MacMichael's Memorandum on Southern Policy, 1930.

British officials in the Sudan also shared an apprehension that Islam was on the march in Africa and it must be checked. In the early 1920s Sir George Schuster, the financial secretary, perceived two forces in Africa: one Arabic and Islamic pressing up the Nile, the other English and Christian moving into the center of the continent from both east and west. British officials feared that, with the improvement of communications, Islam could easily reach their colonies in East Africa.[19] Hence, the Upper Nile regions became battlegrounds for two contesting cultures. Although these attitudes were not formally defined until 1930, the strategy of erecting physical and cultural barriers between North and South began during the first decade of British rule and was translated into hasty and mostly ineffective measures that were not even officially announced at the time.

In 1910 the governor of Mongolla province, R.C.R. Owen, suggested the formation of separate southern army units to substitute for Northern troops serving there. The language of command of the new force would be English and the religious observance Christian. By 1917 an Equatorial Corps composed entirely of Southerners had been formed. Thus a second and related concern was the language question. British Southern officials were instructed by Wingate to encourage the use of English as the language of administration instead of Arabic "without any fuss and without putting the dots too prominently."[20] A clear-cut decision, however, was taken in March 1922, with the consent of the southern governors, that English was to replace Arabic as the language of administration in the South.[21] In the following years, British officials in the districts and provincial headquarters continued quietly to encourage English particularly in missionary schools which were established to provide the necessary training for southern administrative staff. However, the language question in the South remained thoroughly confused even

---

[19]Collins, *Shadows in the Grass*, p. 170.

[20]Collins, *Shadows in the Grass*, p. 167.

[21]N.R.O. Civsec 1/9/31, Civil Secretary's Circular on "Policy in the Southern Sudan," 14 March 1922.

after the Rejaf Conference and was in fact never resolved satisfactorily.

Another attempt at separation was the Passports and Permits Ordinance of 1922, which empowered the civil secretary to declare certain regions of the country as "closed districts" to any Sudanese or foreigner wishing to enter or remain in them. Consequently, the three southern provinces were placed under this category and entry would be by permit only.[22] This was most relevant in the Western District, which shared a border with Darfur that was never effectively controlled. A decision was taken by the southern governors in the late 1920s to remove northern Sudanese mamurs from the South. In view of the acute shortage of administrative personnel, however, this decision was modified and it was decided that northern mamurs should be confined to towns and not be allowed to interfere in the local administration or the proceedings of chiefs' courts.

Thus, MacMichael's memorandum was a masterful summary of the views that had been expressed by previous British administrators and was an embodiment of a policy that had been germinating since the early days of the administration. Nevertheless, the memorandum was the first official document which specified concrete proposals as well as a comprehensive plan for the administration of the South. The new scheme involved first the elimination of all northern human and cultural presence in the South; second, curtailment of any further spread of Arabic and Islamic influences; and third, the "revival" and preservation of traditional cultures. The document contained four major propositions which included the elimination of northern administrative staff and their substitution by Southerners; control of northern traders; British officials familiarization with traditional cultures of southern societies; and finally, the encouragement of English where communication in the local vernacular was not possible.

MacMichael's memorandum provided British officials in the South with an opportunity to carry out what they had been pressing hard to achieve for many years. In the Bahr al-Ghazal Brock became one of the most fervent apostles of the new policy

---

[22]*Sudan Gazette* 402 (15 October 1922).

and proceeded to implement it with the greatest vigor and urgency. To him a long cherished ambition was finally realized.

It should be emphasized that besides Brock there were other figures who played a very crucial role in the application of the Southern Policy. They included Harry Kidd, district commissioner, Western District, and his assistant S.R. Simpson. They were helped by C.G. Dupuis, governor of Darfur Province, and G.D. Lampen, district commissioner, Baqqara. Following receipt of the memorandum, Brock immediately issued detailed instructions to his district commissioners to take the necessary steps to "clean up" their districts. Northern administrators would be removed immediately and northern traders from then on would be screened. Furthermore, the movement of people between the Bahr al-Ghazal and Darfur and Kurdufan provinces was to be prohibited. Although similar steps were taken in the other southern provinces, it was the Western District that became the target and the test of the new policy.

Chapter 4

THE REORGANIZATION OF THE
WESTERN DISTRICT: POPULATION
RESETTLEMENT, 1930-1940

A great deal has been written about the Southern Policy. Most of these writings tend to focus on the implications of that policy on North-South relations. Little attention has been given to its effects on the local people in the Western District where it was rigorously applied. This remote and long neglected area suddenly became the center of government attention and wittnessed the most drastic changes in its recent history. The task of rolling back "foreign" influences from the district involved a total demographic, political, and social restructuring. It resulted in the eviction from the district of a large number of people, perceived as major vehicles through which these "alien" influences were disseminated. This category included northern traders as well as Hausa, Borno, Dajo, Sara, Bergo, and Wadaians. In order to prevent any further spread of northern influences the district had to be sealed off from Darfur and Kurdufan, and physical contact between its inhabitants and those regions was prohibited. Finally, the remaining population of the district was to be moved further south and settled along government roads. The task of implementing this program was entrusted to Captain Kidd and Simpson. However, since the former had gone on leave the early implementation of the program fell upon Simpson.

Northern Traders

The jallaba were the most important group of immigrants. Their presence in this part of the South dates to the eighteenth and nineteenth centuries. Their number increased dramatically after the westward shift of the ivory and slave trade from the White Nile route in the second half of the nineteenth century. After the abolition of the slave trade a considerable number remained in the South and set up small shops, particularly in Bahr al-Ghazal province which was easily accessible via the overland route from Darfur and Kurdufan. In the western Bahr al-Ghazal they settled in Daim al-Zubair, Kafia Kingi, Raga, and Kabaluzu. Although the jallaba came from different parts of the Sudan, they all shared the feature of diaspora trading communities formed in other parts of Africa. They played a very important role in the life of these towns. The most prominent traders in Raga were al-Sayid al-Dishuni, who was appointed by district officials as the Shaikh of the *suq* (market), Ali Muhammad al-Haj, and Hussain Taha. They all came from the riverine regions of the northern Sudan and maintained very close trading connections with their homeland. The jallaba acted as agents and hosts for visiting kinsmen. They provided them with shelter and market information. These traders maintained personal contacts with local rulers, mainly through marriage and facilitating trading connections.[1] These strategic marriages brought advantages both to the jallaba and local rulers. For the former it brought security and access to resources. For the rulers, who were also engaged in long-distance trade, it provided external connections.

British administrators in the South firmly believed that northern Sudanese traders grossly exploited innocent southern customers. Support for this view was readily available from Southerners themselves, among whom traders appear to have been heartily disliked. But unpopularity was an occupational hazard of all immigrant trading communities in all British colonies in Africa. Yet in these other territories prejudice was seldom carried to the point of actually banning the traders. Indeed, the reasons were peculiar to the Sudan. The twentieth century trader was seen as

---

[1]Al-Sharif Muhammad and Ahmad al-Faki for instance married from the family of Nasir Andel, sultan of Nyagulgule, N.R.O. Bahr al-Ghazal Province 1/3/17, Ahmad al-Faki and Al-Sharif Muhammad to Kidd, 8 August 1930.

the successor of the nineteenth century ivory and slave trader. More important, however, the jallaba were perceived as agents of Islamization and Arabicisation. Since they all speak Arabic, the jallaba became very instrumental in the spread of that language in the South.

In line with Southern Policy their removal became the first priority of province officials. Brock had initially intended to expel all of them immediately, but several factors rendered that impossible. The first problem was absence of a readily available substitute and in this respect the Western District was the most unpromising area in the South. The government invoked two strategies for replacement of the jallaba. The first was to encourage Syrian, Lebanese, and Greek merchants. The second was to set up Southerners themselves, with government loans, to establish their own businesses.[2]

However, cautious British officials in Khartoum were abashed at the political consequences that a wholesale expulsion of the jallaba might produce in the North. Consequently MacMichael suggested that "the greatest tact and care will have to be exercised in adjusting means to the end in view."[3] He further requested that detailed information on these merchants, their tribal origins, and whether or not they had any business connections with the big firms in Khartoum, should be obtained before any action was taken. MacMichael urged Brock to proceed with care and give valid justification in each case so that the government could "answer any complaints or inquiries from interested quarters in Khartoum." But the governor was unwilling to compromise his program and assured his assistants that "the Civil Secretary's conditions will not worry us but we must go carefully."[4]

---

[2]N.R.O. Bahr al-Ghazal Province, 1/1/2, Brock to Kidd, 10 June 1930.

[3]N.R.O. Bahr al-Ghazal Province, 1/1/2, MacMichael to Brock, 11 May 1930.

[4]N.R.O. Bahr al-Ghazal Province, 1/3/17, Brock to Kidd, 9 June 1930.

By September 1930 a list of all northern traders in the Western District had been produced. They numbered twenty four—twelve each in Raga and Kafia Kingi. As it turned out, two of them had northern business connections.[5] But both expressed a desire to leave the province. Similarly, fifteen other merchants were prepared to depart and requested financial assistance from the government to do so. These traders were willing to leave voluntarily as their trade had sorely diminished with the curtailment of the ivory and slave trade. The quantity of goods they possessed consisted of minor consumer goods such as clothes and their shops were empty for most of the year.

With the exception of those who had northern connections, Brock was not willing to renew permits to trade in the province. MacMichael had agreed to cancel the permits of those merchants residing at Kafia Kingi on the ground that the town was to be destroyed. He was not prepared, however, to accept a wholesale refusal to renew the permits of those in other parts of the district.[6] The deadline given to the traders was February 1931, after which their permits would expire. Nevertheless, only four merchants were considered "legitimate" by the authorities and were allowed to remain.[7]

---

[5]Those were Mahdi Daifallah and Fadallah al-Shaikh al-Tayyib. Mahdi owned a shop in Daim al-Zubair and was a nephew of a well-known Umdurman-based merchant—Sayid Ahmad Swar al-Dahab. Fadallah owned a shop in Raga and was a brother of Mahdi al-Shaikh al-Tayyib, another well-known merchant in Umdurman. N.R.O. Bahr al-Ghazal Province, 1/3/17, Brock to Civil Secretary, 29 September 1930.

[6]N.R.O. Bahr al-Ghazal Province, 1/3/17, MacMichael to Brock, 22 July 1930.

[7]Those included Mahdi Daifallah in Daim al-Zubair, Fadi Allah al-Shaikh al-Tayyib in Raga, Umar Abd al-Hafiz in Said Bandas; and Sadiq Uthman who was a leather worker.

The West Africans and Awlad al-Arab

The second group to be expelled from the province were immigrants from West Africa, French Equatorial Africa, Darfur, and Kurdufan. They included Hausa, Fulani, and Borno (known as Fellata or Westerners), as well as Sara, Runga, Borgo, Berti, Dajo, Bagirma, just to mention a few. Since the majority of them were Muslims, they were loosely referred to by British officials as "Awlad al-Arab." Their exact number is unknown. A 1930 tax list showed 768 taxpayers. Further lists were compiled in 1931 which gave a total of 2,840 people, of whom 695 were living in Raga and 2,145 in Kafia Kingi.[8]

The majority of these people were concentrated in Kafia Kingi, the ancient commercial center. Situated in the northeastern part of the province on the trade routes from Wadai, Darfur, Kurdufan, and the Chari region, Kafia Kingi had become a commercial town which attracted merchants and peddlers from diverse ethnic and cultural backgrounds. The southern route which passed through it was often used by West Africans who tried to avoid crossing the territory of Ali Dinar. However, after his death in 1916 there had been no need for the pilgrims to make this southern detour. Kafia Kingi had, therefore, become a backwater of the east-west trade routes. The pilgrimage and trade had shifted farther north, passing through Darfur rather than Kafia Kingi. Indeed the northern route offered better facilities and passed through a number of trading centers such as al-Fashir, Nyala, and al-Ubayyid rather than the more difficult territories of the Bahr al-Ghazal. Moreover, this shift coincided with the establishment of the Gezira Scheme, a huge cotton plantation, which attracted a large number of West African immigrants as laborers. In order to ensure the expulsion of these people and prevent their return to the Western District, Brock decided to destroy Kafia Kingi and include it in his famous "no man's land" between Darfur and the Bahr al-Ghazal provinces. The idea was to create a buffer zone to prevent physical contact between the inhabitants of the two

---

[8]N.R.O. Bahr al-Ghazal Province, 1/3/17, Simpson to Brock, 29 April 1931.

provinces. The town would be destroyed and the residents moved to Darfur.

After a series of meetings between the Bahr al-Ghazal and Darfur officials and with Khartoum's approval, it was decided that all these people would be settled in southern Darfur. However, the removal of the West African elements presented a special problem. Early in 1930 MacMichael proposed their settlement in Maiwurno on the Blue Nile or Kassala where they could join their kinsmen who had been living there for several decades. However, Brock and his colleagues in the Bahr al-Ghazal were against this solution, owing to the physical and financial responsiblity it might involve. Darfur was therefore regarded as the most suitable place to which they could be sent. Hence, all the Fellata and Awlad al-Arab were sent to an area between Afifi and Rutrutaya and placed under the umda of the Habbaniya.[9]

The Bandala

The third important category of undesirable elements in the district were the Bandala. As mentioned earlier, the Bandala had taken advantage of their peculiar relationship with the Baqqara and managed to avoid government control. The Bandala were regarded as a nuisance by colonial officials. They were described as "evasive, difficult to catch if criminals, uncontrolled when unlisted and defaulters if listed."[10] Lampen, assistant district commissioner Baqqara District, went on to state: "We have the paradox of a tribe in process of formation, which in face of the government clings resolutely to its theoretical slave status, and clings to it because it finds therein an additional freedom."[11]

As early as the 1920s British officials in the two provinces were trying to find a way to bring the Bandala under government

---

[9]There were reports of starvation and several cases of deaths when these people went to Darfur. N.R.O. Bahr al-Ghazal Province, 1/3/17, Simpson to Brock, 29 April 1930.

[10]AP Box 3/13, Lampen to Governor of Darfur, 18 April 1929.

[11]AP Box 3/13, Lampen to Governor of Darfur, 18 April 1929.

control. In 1929 Simpson and Lampen met in Radom to make plans to place the Bandala in an Omodiya or a chief's court. A few years earlier Hebbert had raised the question of whether it might be possible to force the Baqqara to proclaim all their Madnala free. But all of this was no more than wishful thinking. Now the Southern Policy had created an opportunity and provided a rationale to deal with the so-called Bandala problem once and for all. Since "in speech, religion, and sympathy they were Arabs," their presence in the Western District was against the newly-announced policy.[12] It was decided that all the Bandala should be settled with their ex-masters in Darfur. But the situation was much more complicated. The Bandala system of marriage (referred to in Chapter 2) was a major obstacle to the government's notion of law and order. A Bandalawi could not marry without the consent of his nominal owner, and all the children were considered property of the wife's master. For this reason, there was little intermarriage between the Bandala and the Western District's people who were aware of the fact that the Bandala might take the women and children to their masters in Darfur.[13] Hence, the Bandala have always been regarded as outsiders and could never be integrated into the local communities. Although they are nominally Muslims, the Bandala clinged to their traditional marriage instead of the *sharia* one. Facing this dilemma, British officials decided that in case of a marriage dispute which involved a Bandala and a non-Bandala, the marriage should be treated as a sharia union.[14]

Several plans were discussed desultorily. One of the most intriguing proposals was to invoke the traditional bonds between the Bandala and the Baqqara. "I believe," wrote Simpson, "that I am right in saying that in the north freed slaves are not allowed

---

[12]N.R.O. Bahr al-Ghazal Province, 1/3/17, Simpson to Lampen, 17 May 1930.

[13]AP Box 3/13, Lampen to the Governor of Darfur, 18 April 1929.

[14]AP Box 3/13, Lampen to Governor of Darfur, 18 April 1929.

to leave their tribe, but become a member of it."[15] Hence, the most important goal was to get rid of the Bandala regardless of what effects that decision might have on their social status. However, British officials in Darfur were unwilling to take over what seemed to them a Bahr al-Ghazal problem. They were convinced that the presence of Bandala in their territory would increase the number of "lawless" elements and put an additional burden on their few staff. But after several meetings and pressure from Khartoum, Dupuis, Darfur's governor, agreed to take the Bandala, provided that they would be moved "en bloc" and unarmed.[16] To prevent further contacts between the inhabitants of the two provinces, Brock proposed a buffer zone between Darfur and Bahr al-Ghazal. Although this area would remain nominally a part of the Bahr al-Ghazal, it would be a "no man's land" in which the "Bandala, Ghazalian or Darfurians, and Arabs could roam at will."[17]

These were the official plans. However, their implementation was wrecked by the complex realities of this frontier zone. The Bandala did not want to go to Darfur. Although they wanted to retain their traditional ties with the Baqqara, the Bandala also wanted to maintain their independence by living at a distance from them.[18] Living in Darfur would mean greater control by their masters and make them vulnerable to excessive labor demands. But to colonial officials, the Bandala were "outlaws" and should be brought under government control. In 1930 Simpson encapsulated the dilemma:

> The collection of their poll tax is a matter of the utmost difficulty. They pay or do not pay just as they

---

[15]N.R.O. Bahr al-Ghazal Province, 1/3/17, Simpson to Lampen, 9 May 1930.

[16]N.R.O. Bahr al-Ghazal Province, 1/3/17, Dupuis to Brock, 7 November 1930.

[17]The southern limit of the buffer zone was fixed at latitude 8-45 n. N.R.O. Bahr al-Ghazal Province, 1/3/17, Brock to Kidd, 9 June 1930.

[18]Interview with Ali Duluma, 14 July 1987.

please. Indeed it is really only the old men who can be relied on. The young men who ought to pay or work in lieu of payment, are always reported as "having gone to Darfur"or if found here "they have only just returned." Each year's list varies from the previous year's, there being a large number of arrivals and departures.[19]

The deadline passed and no Bandala had arrived in Kogul, their new site in southern Darfur. Simpson was ready to burn their huts in the Bahr al-Ghazal, and Rowland, the district commissioner in Darfur, was prepared to send his police to round them up.[20] The Bandala removal dragged on for another year with no results. Those who went to Darfur in 1930 had returned to the Bahr al-Ghazal complaining about their ex-masters. Simpson was convinced that their grievances were greatly exaggerated and he was therefore determined to allow no permanent settlement of the Bandala in the Western District. Consequently, they were told that they could remain in the Bahr al-Ghazal until the dry season and then they would have to go.

In July 1933 the situation appeared to be far from satisfactory: of the estimated 498 Bandala listed in Kafia Kingi in 1929 tax lists, only 30 had arrived in Darfur.[21] At this point, D.J. Bethell, the new district commissioner Western District, was ready to use the army to round them up. But despite numerous warnings and threats, the Bandala chiefs flatly refused to go to Darfur and continued to pursue their way of life of fishing, hunting, and collecting honey. Realizing the futility of their efforts, British officials decided to seek the cooperation of the Feroge and Nyagulgule chiefs to use their influence over the Bandala. Yet this

---

[19]N.R.O. Bahr al-Ghazal Province, 1/3/17, Simpson to Lampen 17 May 1930.

[20]N.R.O. Bahr al-Ghazal Province, 1/3/17, Simpson to Brock, 29 April 1931. Rowland died a month later in Buram of blackwater fever.

[21]N.R.O. Bahr al-Ghazal Province, 1/3/17, Dupuis to Brock, 5 May 1933.

strategy did not yield any results. Colonial officials did not run out of ideas: if the Bandala could not be moved, certainly the province borders could. Although initially reluctant, the governor of Darfur agreed to move his province boundary further south. However, Ingelson, the new governor of Bahr al-Ghazal, preferred the retention of Brock's no-man's land. The two governors agreed to conduct frequent patrols and keep the Bandala north of the Bahr al-Arab. However, these decisions remained notional and it was finally decided that these people should be left alone.

Internal Relocation

The Southern Policy provided British officials in the Western District with an opportunity to integrate this remote area effectively into the colonial system and bring its population under government control. The majority of people of the Western District were dispersed over a wide area, in relatively isolated pockets and far away from administrative centers. Just as the evacuation of "unwanted" elements was taking place, provincial officials were laboriously engaged in transferring the remaining population from their villages and settling them further south along government roads. The entire population of the district was assembled on these roads, forming several settlements. In arranging these settlements, primary consideration was given to linguistic, religious, and ethnic affinities.

In this respect Muslim groups such as the Feroge, Indiri, Shaiu, Nyagulgule, and Mangayat were ordered to settle along the Raga-Aweil road to the northeast of Raga.[22] The 1929 tax list showed eight hundred Feroge taxpayers. They had lived in and around Raga for several decades. They were now ordered to move four miles to the northeast of the town.[23] The Nyagulgule were asked to move from their home near Telgona to Kabaluzu.

---

[22]See map.

[23]N.R.O. Bahr al-Ghazal Province, 1/3/17, Kidd to Brock, 8 August 1930.

The next major settlement was along the Raga-Said Bandas road, to the west of Raga. This became the new home for the Kreish, Binga, Kara, and the Yulu. The Kreish were the largest ethnic group in the district, numbering approximately 2,500 tax-payers. Most writers have concluded that the Kreish had once lived in Darfur. Threatened by successive waves of slave traders, they drifted to the south and scattered in the border region between the Sudan and today's Central African Republic. As a result of al-Sanusi's attacks, a large number fled to the Bahr al-Ghazal, forming three sections corresponding to their clans: the Naka, Ndogo, and Hufra. Due to their proximity to Darfur, the ruling family of the Hufra section had paid tribute to the sultanate and were heavily Islamized. The Naka and Ndogo sections had lived around Said Bandas and Daim al-Zubair respectively. Despite the animosity among the leaders of these three clans, they were lumped together along the Raga-Said Bandas road.[24] This settlement also included the Aja, Binga, and Kara. The settlement of the last two groups created a dilemma for colonial officials and will be dealt with later.

The third important settlement was to the southeast of Raga, along the Raga-Daim al-Zubair road. This included the Banda, Belanda, Shatt, and a few Azande immigrants. The Banda comprised the bulk of this settlement. Almost all the Banda had come from French Equatorial Africa in response to al-Sanusi's raids and the French policies of taxation and forced labor. The Belanda and the few Zande immigrants were placed under one chief. British officials then had to face the problem of settling "displaced" elements. This category included discharged soldiers, emancipated slaves, and other dislocated people. They were all settled in Raga.

This massive compulsory movement involved approximately 5,258 households. For some groups it meant a minor move; but for others it meant traveling a long distance and a complete change of habitat. The Kreish for instance had to walk 350 kilometers. Some Bandas had to walk from Kafia Kingi to Raga.

---

[24]This was indeed the case of Musa Komondogo and Said Bandas.

Binga and Kara Defiance

Not all the people of the Western District accepted their fate. One of the most daunting problems that faced colonial officials was settlement of the Binga and Kara. As with the Feroge and Nyagulgule, the ruling dynasties of the Kara had a tradition of foreign origin. They claimed that their ancestors had once lived in Sinnar on the Blue Nile around the seventeenth century. Afterwards they migrated to Jabal Marra in Darfur, from which they had drifted south to the Bahr al-Ghazal where they split and formed two settlements, one on the Yata River and the other to the west of Jali.[25] Both sections paid tribute to the Fur sultan. During the nineteenth century, the Kara were raided by al-Zubair, the Mahdists, and the Kreish. At the beginning of this century many of them were enslaved by Ali Dinar and were taken to Darfur. In 1927 it was estimated that there were 254 Kara taxpayers divided between two chiefs.

The Binga held traditions similar to those of the Kara, which indicated an eastern origin. After a sojourn in Jabal Marra, they had migrated south and ended up in the Bahr al-Ghazal. The Binga inhabited the mountains on the Nile-Chari divide to the west of Kafia Kingi. They comprised five clans that were scattered in the Sudan-Central African Republic border region. Their history was similar to that of the Kara and they had also been subjugated by the Fur sultans. They were further victimized and enslaved by Ali Dinar and al-Sanusi of Dar al-Kuti at the beginning of this century. After the defeat of Ali Dinar in 1916 they returned to the Bahr al-Ghazal, where their settlements in the Western District were estimated at 374 taxpayers in 1927. The two groups exhibit close linguistic and cultural affinities. Due to their long history of contacts with Darfur, some of them had been Islamized but a large number remained animist. Their links with Darfur continued during the condominium period. Many of their kinsmen resided in Darfur and a significant number still go there seeking employment.

According to official classification, the Binga and Kara were "pagan negro tribes" and should, therefore, be settled with the rest

---

[25]Santandrea, *Tribal History*, pp. 240-43.

of the district's population.[26] Beside the goal of bringing them under control, there were other reasons for this strategy. The Binga and Kara visits to Darfur would allow them to "indulge in their favorite pastime of brawling with Arab grazing parties," which was against the Southern Policy.[27]

Just as the Bandala had refused to go north, two sections of the Binga and Kara made every possible effort not to go south. As early as 1931, during the heyday of the population reshuffle, a number of chiefs appeared in Zalengi in Darfur province and declared that they wanted to settle there. They were asked to move back to the Bahr al-Ghazal. A month later they appeared again in Buram and were joined by other drifters. Captain Kidd sent his police to burn their huts and the Binga were sent back to the Bahr al-Ghazal.[28] Despite these actions about one hundred and fifty people scattered in the area of Radom in southeastern Darfur. In January 1932, Darfur police arrested sixty-seven Binga and handed them over to the Western District authorities. A few months later they returned to the same place. British officials understood the Binga and Kara's attitude as defiance. But the migration of these people to Darfur was motivated by several factors. The economically depressed Western District had very little to offer, while Darfur presented a better opportunity for wage-earning jobs. Moreover, Darfur was less demanding in terms of tribute payment and labor requisition.[29]

In April 1932 Madden and Simpson met at Safaha to discuss their strategy to expel the Binga and Kara from Darfur. One of the options discussed was to prevent their using the water resources in the area and generally "make life unpleasant for

---

[26]N.R.O. Bahr al-Ghazal Province, 1/6/36, Notes on a meeting between Maden and Simpson at Safaha, 11 April 1932.

[27]N.R.O. Bahr al-Ghazal Province, 1/6/36, Notes on a meeting between Maden and Simpson at Safaha, 11 April 1932.

[28]N.R.O. Bahr al-Ghazal Province, 1/6/36, Kidd to Brock, 14 March 1931.

[29]Interview with Adam Kuvolo, 24 October 1984.

them."[30] But owing to the fear that this action might prompt them to move to the French territories, this strategy was not pursued. Hence, it was decided that these people should be rounded up by police from both districts. Meanwhile, it was reported that a large number of Binga and Kara were starving in southern Darfur. The governor of Darfur suggested that they should be offered a domicile "somewhere" north of the Bahr al-Arab. But the Bahr al-Ghazal officials were not willing to compromise their plans. From now on the matter became a subject of a heated debate between the authorities of the two provinces. Brock and his staff were convinced that the problem could not be resolved without active participation from Darfur. Dupuis, however, had no staff to spare and the Binga-Kara affair dragged on.

By the middle of 1932, the Binga and the Kara were still scattered in the border region and there were even reports that some of them had gone to al-Fashir and the French territories.[31] In March 1933, Bethell, district commissioner Western District and Crawford, district commissioner Southern Darfur, met at Safaha to arrange the return of some fifty people who took refuge with Faki Nur al-Din of the Habbaniyah. Bethell wanted them to be arrested and sent back to the Bahr al-Ghazal. But in a rather revealing statement Crawford replied: "They differ in no respect from other Awlad al-Arab."[32]

A whole year passed and no progress was made. Finally Khartoum intervened. Gillan, the civil secretary, proposed a plan to alter the boundaries between the two provinces.[33] By the redrawing of the boundary, the Binga and Kara could easily have

---

[30]N.R.O. Bahr al-Ghazal Province, 1/6/36, Notes on a meeting between Maden and Simpson, 11 April 1932.

[31]N.R.O. Bahr al-Ghazal Province, 1/6/36, Resume of action taken in regard to the Binga Kara.

[32]N.R.O. Bahr al-Ghazal Province, 1/6/36, Resume of action taken in regard to the Binga Kara.

[33]N.R.O. Bahr al-Ghazal Province, 1/3/17, Gillan to Dupuis, 1 May 1934.

been transferred to the Bahr al-Ghazal, while the Bandala could come under Darfur. But these proposals were opposed by Ingelson, the new governor of the Bahr al-Ghazal, who insisted that these people should be returned. A year latter, he was transferred to become the governor of Darfur. Martin Parr succeeded him as governor of a newly-created province of Equatoria which was an amalgam of the Bahr al-Ghazal and Mongalla provinces. Paradoxically, Ingelson, who had pressed very hard for the return of the Binga and Kara to the Bahr al-Ghazal, now become less committed to the idea. This attitude had resulted in stormy relations between him and Martin Parr who believed that Darfur should use every possible means, including force, to evict the Binga and Kara. When Darfur refused to cooperate, Parr did not hesitate to send his police on several occasions to burn the Binga and Kara settlements in that province. These actions met with Ingelson's incredulity. He wrote to Parr: "The Bahr al-Ghazal behaved with unjustified ruthlessness."[34] Parr was furious and wrote back asserting that "southern tribes should live in the South and not in the Northern Sudan."[35] Throughout the year, the two governors were embroiled in a heated exchange with a voluminous correspondence which produced no results.

Finally Khartoum officials, who were far removed from an issue which preoccupied their colleagues on the spot, decided to intervene. Addressing the two governors, the civil secretary wrote: "After consideration of the history and circumstances of the case, His Excellency, the Governor General has directed that these Binga and Kara are not to be evicted from Darfur."[36] Moreover, they were to be settled under some tribal chief, but "should not be recognized as a tribal unit." Thus, after six years of harassment, the Binga and Kara were left alone.

---

[34]N.R.O. Bahr al-Ghazal Province, 1/6/36, Ingelson to Parr, 10 December 1936.

[35]N.R.O. Bahr al-Ghazal Province, 1/6/36, Parr to Ingelson, 17 December 1936.

[36]N.R.O. Bahr al-Ghazal Province, 1/6/36, Gillan to Governors Bahr al-Ghazal and Darfur Provinces, 1 February 1937.

A great deal of attention was given to the Bahr al-Ghazal and Darfur border and the prohibition of contacts between the inhabitants of the two provinces. This question had absorbed successive officials of the two provinces since the early 1920s. This is one of the most complex frontiers in the Sudan. One of the most difficult issues was the southward movement of the Baqqara to trade and graze south of the Bahr al-Arab and the northward movement of Bandala, Kreish, Binga, and the Kara. In 1930 Brock and Dupuis agreed that Darfur people could bring their cattle to the Bahr al-Ghazal, and the Kreish could go to Darfur.[37] Brock, however, insisted that the southern limit of Baqqara grazing should be at a line drawn from Kafia Kingi in the west, passing through Jabal Ambusu and Jabal Airi, to Jabal Tambeli in the east.[38]

The frontier question became more pressing because of the Bandala, Binga and Kara quandary. In 1934, the civil secretary suggested a change in the boundary between the two provinces, but Bahr al-Ghazal officials preferred the existing border. The authorities of the two provinces, however, agreed to share the task of policing and guarding the "no man's land." A permit system was introduced in 1935. Accordingly, all border-crossing without written permission from the district commissioner was illegal. More measures were introduced the late 1930s and early 1940s. Intermarriage between the people of Darfur and the Bahr al-Ghazal was prohibited. To enforce these rules, robust measures such as imprisonment and deportation were introduced. However, in view of the reality of this frontier zone and the lack of sufficient personnel these rules remained notional.

---

[37]N.R.O. Bahr al-Ghazal Province, 1/1/12, Notes on the Western District, 1935.

[38]N.R.O. Bahr al-Ghazal Province, 1/1/12, Notes on the Western District, 1935.

Chapter 5

WESTERN BAHR AL-GHAZAL
AND THE "NEW DEAL"

By 1932, the physical aspect of the government's program was accomplished. "Undesirable" elements were evicted and, with the exception of the Binga and Kara, the remaining population of the district had settled in their new places along roads. At the end of the year, Simpson was transferred to al-Damir in the northern Sudan and the district was taken over by David Bethell. In brief, what was thought to be a prerequisite for the revival of traditional culture, effective administration, and economic development, had been created.

The Administrative Framework

The entire population of the district was organized into five chiefs' courts. The composition of these courts was determined by ethnic and linguistic considerations. In the far west, two sections of the Kreish as well as the Aja were placed under Said Bandas's court, with a population of 1,480 taxpayers. Next to it was the Minamba (known later as Parapara) court. Its 967 subjects included the Binga, Kara, Yulu, and a few Kreish. The Muslim groups of Feroge, Indiri, Shaiu, and the Nyagulgule were placed under the Gossinga court, with 1,063 subjects. The smaller groups such as the Belanda, Biviri, and Shatt, numbering 846 taxpayers, were lumped together under the Kuru court. The large settlement of 1,495 Banda immigrants and the Mangayat were assembled under a court that was simply designated Court 25.[1]

---

[1]*Equatoria Handbook*, vol. 2, Sudan Government Publication, 1949.

This arrangement was meant to foster the progress of native administration in the district. But as it turned out, the southward movement of the district's population had created enormous administrative and social problems. "Although it made a neater tribal grouping," remarked Simpson "it was in any view a move in the wrong direction i.e. further away from province headquarters in Wau."[2] Indeed, this was a sound criticism considering the poor communication and the absence of all-season roads between Wau and Raga. The Kreish, for instance, were now 70 miles from Raga and 277 miles from Wau.

Efforts initiated to foster native rule were wrecked by a host of factors. The functioning of these courts was frustrated by the diversity of their subjects and the lack of a common language. Court records were kept either in English, Arabic, or the language of the dominant group in the court. The records of the Gossinga court for example were kept in Arabic. As far as other courts were concerned, British officials and the missionaries could not agree on whether to use Kapala (the Kreish language) or Nodogo. This conflict was more prevalent in the Kuru court where the missionaries insisted on the use of Ndogo while British officials pressed for the use of Kapala.

There was a constant conflict between traditional customs and government's ideals in regard to marriage, adultery, and witchcraft. The list of acts regarded as criminal offences increased as the government continued to impose new rules regarding game hunting, possession of firearms, local brewering of *araqi*, hashish smoking and so forth.[3] This led to a great deal of confusion and abuses. People were imprisoned and whipped for commiting acts which they did not understand to be punishable.

Amalgamation and rearrangement of courts became a common practice in the 1930s. The original courts were designated "B" courts and given increasing responsibility by being allowed to give greater penalties of up to two years imprisonment, twenty five

---

[2]SAD 720/4, Simpson's Papers.

[3]In 1939 for instance, there were 71 non-summary and 140 summary convictions. SAD 710/7, Western District Annual Report, 1939.

piastres fine, and twenty lashes. Below the "B" courts a large number of "A" courts had been founded to grant minor sentences –up to three months imprisonment, two piastres fine, and ten lashes. Hence, the "B" courts became courts of appeal. This was the theory, but in reality public security was still dependent upon the district commissioner. He supervised the courts, kept accounts, and collected taxes. The courts' powers were constantly reduced. Moreover, the authority of traditional rulers was circumscribed by colonial officials. Influential chiefs were despised and were targeted by the officials. Chiefs were often dismissed if they failed to perform their duties to the district commissioner's satisfaction. In 1939 two prominent chiefs in the district were dismissed: Ngsanga of the Bor Belanda for "maladministration," and Bandi of the Banda for involvement in the activities of secret societies. In February 1940 Babikir Said Bandas, chief of Kreish-Naka was dismissed for his "complicity" in the killing of an old woman. In the same year, Kosho Jajugu, another Kreish chief, and Tinyang of the Shatt were dismissed and imprisoned, the latter for setting free persons sentenced to imprisonment by the Kuru court.[4] Traditional leaders had to be obsequious to retain their posts. However, one of the most serious confrontations with colonial authorities took place in the mid 1930s and involved Isa Ahmad Fartak, the Feroge sultan.

As mentioned earlier, the ruling dynasty of the Feroge had claimed a Borno origin and maintained strong links with the Fur sultanate. The claim of "noble descent" and linkage with Darfur has always been emphasized by the ruling family who kept charters and genealogies which confirmed that they were descendants of a Borno pilgrim.[5] While the ruling family was thoroughly Islamized

[4]SAD 710/10, Western District Annual Report 1940-41. Simpson was astonished when one of his policemen crawled on his knees to the great sultan Jallab of the Yulu. He could not believe that a local leader could have such influence over his subjects. SAD 720/4, Simpson's Papers.

[5]Stefano Santandrea, "A preliminary Account of the Indiri, Togoyo, Feroge, Mangayat, and Woro," *Sudan Notes and Records* 34 (1953): 230-44.

and fluent in Arabic, their subjects (such as Indiri and Shaiu) spoke Kaligi and remained nominally Muslims.

Isa's father, Ahmad Fartak, was captured by the Mahdists when they invaded this area and was taken to Umdurman where he later fought against the Anglo-Egyptian forces at Karari in 1898. Following the defeat of the Mahdists, he fled to Darfur and thence to Raga. In 1908 Ahmad Fartak was appointed by the government as the Feroge sultan after the dismissal of his brother Musa Hamid. After Ahmad's death in 1926, his son Isa became the new sultan.[6] Isa assumed leadership of the Feroge at the height of native administration which confirmed and supported the position of traditional rulers and enabled them to retain authority while simultaneously pursuing wealth and power under the colonial system. Although the ruling family of the Feroge had always collected tribute from their subjects, the colonial system created new sources of wealth such as regularized salaries and remuneration from tribute collection. Isa was regarded as one of the main "collaborators" in the district. He was literate in Arabic and in the early 1930s was appointed a Third Class Magistrate and president of the Raga court. Simpson described him as "very useful on Courts. He possesses balance and sound judgment."[7] Isa impressed the colonial officials and was awarded a Second Class Belt of Honor in 1935.

However, the announcement of the Southern Policy and the measures taken by the government presented a threat to Isa's interests. The campaign against Arabic and Islam presented a challenge to the fundamental basis of his rule and deprived him of a principal source of legitimacy and prestige. Isa resented the removal of the Bandala, Borno, and Kreish from his jurisdiction; the government's attempt to remove him from Raga; and most important, the educational and cultural policies that were introduced in the district in the wake of the Southern Policy. He

---

[6]N.R.O. Bahr al-Ghazal Province, 1/3/17, Note by D.J. Bethell, 12 March 1936.

[7]N.R.O. Bahr al-Ghazal Province, 1/3/17, Note by D.J. Bethell, 12 March 1936.

opposed removal of the Borno to whom the Feroge traced their ancestry. The Borno fakis (Quranic teachers) were also involved in religious teaching in the district. The expulsion of these elements reduced his sphere of authority and deprived him of a very important source of income in the form of taxes and other dues. For instance, there were at least 183 Kreish taxpayers under Isa who were moved and settled under their own independent sultans.

Government actions resulted not only in the demographic restructuring of the Western District but also in the redistribution of political power. In this respect the government tried to bolster the Kreish as the leading political entity in the district. Although the Kreish were the largest single ethnic group in the western Bahr al-Ghazal, yet until recently they do not seem to have had a sense of political or cultural unity. In fact the term Kreish was applied to them by foreigners. The Kreish occupied a vast area extending from Daim al-Zubair in the south to Kafia Kingi in the north, and across the border in French Equatorial Africa. Threatened by the attacks of slave traders, the Kreish drifted to the south and southwest where they settled in the eastern part of the Chari Basin. As a result of al-Sanusi's raids, a large number fled back to the east where they scattered in the western part of the Bahr al-Ghazal. Although some of them became Muslims (especially the Hufra) the majority of the Kreish remained animists. In view of the preponderance of animism among them, the Kreish were viewed by the missions as potential converts. To British officials the Kreish could serve as a bulwark against northern influences: "Politically the aim was to create in the Western District a solid block capable of resisting Northern influences and for this purpose Kreish is the obvious tribe to build on."[8] The Naka were described as "intelligent and industrious people" and the Ndogo as "decent and orderly."[9] Despite hostilities between their leaders, all the Kreish were assembled along the

---

[8]N.R.O. Bahr al-Ghazal Province, 1/2/11, Ingleson Report, 1935.

[9]N.R.O. Bahr al-Ghazal Province, 1/3/17, Simpson to Brock, 2 June 1931.

Raga-Said Bandas road to "shield" the district from Darfur. This move was resented by the Kreish who, as late as 1939, were expressing a desire to return to Kafia Kingi and the Bahr al-Arab region. Furthermore, British officials made every possible attempt to make Kapala, the Kreish language, the lingua franca in the district.

The elevation of the Kreish was highly resented by Isa Fartak and the ruling family of the Feroge who had always considered themselves the leading nobility in this region. Isa did not hide his resentment. In May 1930 Isa wrote to Simpson as follows:

> If the government really wanted that everyone return to his country of origin, it should have ordered Sultans Azrag, Adam Yango, Said Bandas and Barud Nimir to return to the French Congo whence they recently came (nine or ten years ago). They are from there. This country does not belong to them, it belongs to the Shaiu, Indiri, Mangyat, Shatt, the Kreish of Daim al-Zubair, and the Kreish Hufra.[10]

In February 1931, Isa wrote to Amir Abd al-Hamid of Zalingei seeking asylum as a result of what he regarded as "government hostility towards Islam."[11] Early in October 1930 seven Feroge shaikhs wrote to Brock requesting the attachment of the Feroge to Darfur, but their request was categorically denied. All the Feroge and their subjects were ordered to move from Raga, the historic seat of their rule, to Khor Shammam, a move they sullenly resented. In addition to the fact that Khor Shammam was considered a place of exile for Isa, it was also very close to the Shatt who had been antagonistic to the Feroge for at least two generations. As a result of Simpson's threat to burn down his

---

[10]N.R.O. Bahr al-Ghazal Province, 1/3/17, Isa Fartak to D.C. Western District, 30 May 1930.

[11]N.R.O. Bahr al-Ghazal Province, 1/3/17, Isa to Amir Abd al-Hamid, 1 February 1931.

residence Isa reluctantly left Raga and continued his resistance from Khor Shammam.

Another important factor in Isa's case was the personal animosity between him and Bethell. Although the district commissioner was impressed by Isa's performance in the chiefs' courts, yet he described him as "bloody-minded" and regarded him as a major threat to government policy.[12] Isa's persistence in denouncing the Southern Policy and his resistance to the introduction of missionary education in the district led finally to his dismissal in 1937. He was replaced by his brother Tamim Fartak. Isa was exiled to Yei and finally to al-Fashir where he remained until 1956 when he was reinstated as sultan. But with the exception of Isa's opposition and the defiance of the Binga and Kara, the majority of the people in the western Bahr al-Ghazal had quietly settled in their new locations.

Like the rest of the South the fortunes of the Western District were affected by the economic realities of the time. The economic crisis of the thirties which coincided with Sir Stewart Symes' policy of "care and maintenance" had an adverse impact on the region. In the heyday of the Southern Policy, the Bahr al-Ghazal and Mongalla provinces were amalgamated in 1936 to form Equatoria province. The measure was especially aimed at cutting the number of personnel and reducing the cost of administration. In Symes's view, the government could not afford more than twenty-three officials of whom three would be stationed at the province headquarters, leaving twenty men distributed among eleven districts and covering an area of two hundred thousand square miles. Moreover, and in line with the new policy, Ingelson decided to abolish the double inspectorate system which had been adopted since the First World War, and instead station a single officer in each district. However, the system remained in effect in some districts.

At the same time, the small Central District with its headquarters at Wau was amalgamated with the Western District, thereby forming a huge administrative unit of 38,000 square miles

---

[12]N.R.O. Bahr al-Ghazal Province, 1/3/17, Bethell to Brock, 10 June 1934.

with a population of 83,000 people. Raga was reduced to a mere police post. In Ingelson's view, this area did not justify more than one political officer. But this was contingent upon the completion of an all-season road from Wau to Raga. Yet, just as funds were not available for staff recruitment, they were not available for road construction. Road building had to be delayed without the necessary £3,800 which was never appropriated.

Reduction of the already small staff meant further neglect for the Western District. The people of Raga were nearly twice as far from the district headquarters in Wau as the people of Kafia Kingi had been from Raga. The district commissioner had to travel to Raga to collect taxes and do all the paper work. Raga was marginalised and the administration's attention now focused on Wau. Initially Symes had intended to eliminate Wau as the province headquarters. This was vehemently opposed by Ingleson who argued for the administrative and commercial importance of the town.

Following the amalgamation of the two districts, Wau was "defined as a trading center and government post." In the late 1930s, the provincial authorities embarked on a grand scheme of "reorganizing" the town. Reorganization in those days meant evictions and compulsory population movement. In their effort to "reorganize" Wau, the province officials followed the footsteps of their predecessors—Brock, Kidd, and Simpson. The inhabitants of Wau were classified into two categories: "legitimate" residence and "undesirable" elements. The latter included immigrants from northern and western Sudan, and elements from West Africa. They were all considered "dangerous to public security" and should therefore be removed to the North. According to officials, this measure intended to achieve "controlling vagabondage, reducing violence, effective collection of taxes etc." and to make Wau a "healthy and well-administered government and trading station."[13] The remaining people were grouped into "tribal" quarters, known as the Native Lodging. Retired-soldiers and police were given the choice either to live in their tribal quarters or leave to their homes. Immigration into town was prohibited and chiefs were

---

[13]SAD 710/7, Western District Annual Report, 1939.

required to report any newcomers. In this regard the Dinka were specifically targeted to keep Nilotes out of Wau. This measure was reinforced by raising the poll tax in Wau from thirty to forty piastres, the highest in the country. An empty area of five miles radus around town was kept as a buffer zone. Chiefs were urged to prevent vagabondage in their quarters. Squatters, beer-brewers, and the a labor camp which was created during the Second World War, were kept outside the buffer zone. The Muslim community of Wau was organized under the mamur, Muhammad Ahmad Abu al-Dahab, who had single-handedly implemented the reorganization. They were urged to keep their society free of people who "while claiming the priviledge of Islam, were either ignorant of or unwilling to undertake the obligations of true Muslims."[14] As a result Wau lost more than one third of its population. In 1937 the population of Wau was 1553 taxpayers (heads of households); by 1941, it was reduced to 1164.[15]

During the war years district commissions came and went with increasing frequency. Each had his own views about the "Southern Policy." Between 1938 and June 1940, B. Brown was district commissioner of the Western District. In July 1940 C.B. Tracy was transferred from Yei to Wau, as assistant district commissioner. He was promoted to deputy governor of the Blue Nile and left Wau in October 1940.[16]

In December 1940 G.L. Elliot-Smith was appointed as district commissioner in the Western District. The new district commissioner had much to ask about Southern Policy, its essence, and purpose. "More detailed direction is now required," he wrote to Martin Parr, "with as little secrecy as possible."[17] The governor responded by stating: "The issue is separation until the South is

---

[14]SAD 710/7, Western District Report, 1939.

[15]In 1937 the population of Wau was estimated at 1,553 people; by 1942 there were only 934. SAD 710/7, Western District Report, 1939.

[16]SAD 7/10, Western District Annual Report, 1940-41.

[17]N.R.O. Bahr al-Ghazal Province, 1/1/2, Elliot-Smith to Martin Parr, 9 April 1941.

strong enough to stand upon its own feet and to develop in accordance with its own ethos."[18] The new district commissioner had vainly argued for Southern economic development as the only way of helping the region to stand on its feet. He understood the Southern Policy as a scheme of rigorous separation from the north. Elliot-Smith was not willing to tolerate any contacts between inhabitants of the Western District and those of Darfur because "whether an Arab comes to hunt or graze or preach Islam or trade, he is spreading Northern influences."[19]

Elliot-Smith maintained that Daim al-Zubair should become the headquarter of the Western District. To this effect he suggested removal of all people living to the west of Raga to the Kuru and Biri rivers. Such a move, he hoped, "could widen the gap between the Southern tribes and Darfur thus furthering the policy of separation." The concentration of people in one area, in his view, could also facilitate introduction of "village industries" such as communal oil presses and handicrafts. To implement both the executive and developmental aspects of these recommendations district headquarters should be moved from Wau to Daim al-Zubair.

Elliot Smith launched a massive attack on the measures that were taken in previous years, especially staff reduction. "In brief—west of Wau, there is *no staff at all* senior to the Sergeant Major at Raga and the D.C. on trek must do literally every thing."[20] The problem was compounded by the reorganization of the old courts. Their authority was cut down, from two-to-three years imprisonment to six months. Sub-chiefs were abolished and replaced by group leaders, thereby multiplying the number of representatives with whom the district commissioner must deal. Elliot-Smith lamented that

[18]N.R.O. Bahr al-Ghazal Province, 1/1/2, Elliot-Smith to Martin Parr, 9 April 1941.

[19]N.R.O. Bahr al-Ghazal Province, 1/1/2, Elliot-Smith to Martin Parr, 9 April 1941.

[20]N.R.O. Bahr al-Ghazal Province, 1/1/2, Elliot-Smith to Martin Parr, 9 April 1941.

Something is badly wrong here. Such an overwhelming amount of petty (though essential) detail now has to be done by the D.C. in person that his proper functions are endangered: the highly paid foreigner is "doing the job himself" rather than supervising Africans learning to help themselves. He is not only the motive power but the whole Government machine: if he stops every thing comes to standstill.[21]

Elliot-Smith not only argued for an increase in personnel but also stressed the need for a Southern staff capable of relieving British district commissioners of their petty duties.

The Southern Policy devolved, in part, from a desire to conserve funds and personnel by entrusting native administration to traditional rulers and create a new southern administrative staff but "perhaps the most disappointing aspect of the working of the Southern Policy is the failure to produce in ten years any Southern staff trained for executive work." He suggested the creation of a new category of administrators whom he termed "Southern Station Officers."

Elliot-Smith could not understand how that district (Western District) could be run from Wau. He suggested that Wau should be attached to Tonj and become the headquarters of "an all-Dinka" district, owing to the links between Wau and the Bahr al-Ghazal Dinka. In a long letter to the governor, Elliot-Smith outlined his proposals and came up with all sorts of justifications for the separation of the Western District from Wau:

An all-Dinka district may have a quarter of a million "Gentle Savages," but they all speak the same language and have the same customs, and their strong character and tribal cohesion is an insulation against northern influence. Western District has only 60,000 to 80,000 inhabitants but they are divided among some 14 different languages. The nine court centers deal with

---

[21]N.R.O. Bahr al-Ghazal Province, 1/1/2, Elliot-Smith to Parr, 30 June 1941.

intertribal cases of amazing complexity due to the different customs of the tribes involved. Mandala nominal rolls and Darfur Frontier Passes entail a closeness of administration unique in Equatoria. The only existing lingua franca is the "Arabic" [sic] forbidden by this Southern Policy which dominates and complicates the whole, for here in Western District the position is not that of defending a naturally strong position but of resuscitating a position which has already fallen. To change the metaphor–it requires more work to pump water uphill than to guide its natural flow. Arabian influence has breached the natural channel of Western District's tribal development and the leak has spread to a veritable slough of despond [sic]. We have set ourselves no less a task than to pump it back, and dam the breach, and guide the channel to a better outlet. The pump must be manned.[22]

Elliot-Smith could not convince his colleagues and his proposals were rejected and became one of the reasons for his removal. The province governor saw things differently. Following reorganization of Wau in 1939-1940, only a hundred Dinka remained in the town as opposed to 1,360 other people, of whom 114 were West Africans, and 120 Azande; many were jallaba. Moreover, the Roman Catholic Mission which was in charge of Western District education, had its headquarters in Wau.

Elliot-Smith was transferred to Abyssinia in June 1941. D.M.H. Evans, the assistant district commissioner at the time became district commissioner and E.J. Bickersteth arrived as assistant district commissioner in August 1941. Evans took a position opposite to his predecessor's. He was against the idea of attaching Wau to the Tonj District. In his view, Wau had 1360 non-Dinka residents as opposed to the 100 Dinka. He firmly believed that application of the Southern Policy in the Tonj and

---

[22]N.R.O. Bahr al-Ghazal Province, 1/1/2, Elliot-Smith to Parr, 30 June 1941.

Western districts was different. He wrote: "The Dinka are Nilotes and different from the farmers of the Congo Basin. They had a common language, and they had not been administered until late." The people of the Western District were scattered and had diverse ethnic background and were generally "docile" and vunerable to Northern influences.[23] He emphasized the objectives of Southern Policy as stated by MacMichael ten years previously.

Nonetheless, by the end of 1941 what his predecessor had argued for was achieved: Wau was transferred to the Tonj District and Raga once again became the headquarters of the Western District. Evans was transferred in the middle of 1942. He was followed by a number of district commissioners who did not stay long enough to effect any significant change in the district. Moreover, growing nationalism in the North had changed the political climate in the country and prompted the government to review its policy in the South. Almost ten years after the amalgamation of Mongalla and the Bahr al-Ghazal, it was finally realized that this action had hindered the progress of administration and inhibited economic development. Hence, it was decided that Equatoria province should be redivided. This was in 1944. However, redivision was not fully undertaken until January 1946 when T.R.H. Owen was appointed as deputy governor; two years later he became the governor of the Bahr al-Ghazal.

In the late 1940s the Southern Policy became a low priority and finally vanished in the dust of pre-independence politics. On 16 December 1946 Sir James Robertson, the civil secretary, informed the governor of Equatoria, B.V. Marwood, that henceforth all planning would be predicated on the union of the South and the North.[24] The first northern Sudanese district commissioner in the Western District was 'Uthman Ali al-Naw.

---

[23]N.R.O. Bahr al-Ghazal Province, 1/1/2, Evans to the Governor, January 1941.

[24]N.R.O. Bahr al-Ghazal Province, 1/1/2, J.W. Robertson's Statement on Southern Policy, 16 December 1946.

Economic and Social Development

One of the declared objectives of the Southern Policy was separating the South until the "region is strong enough to stand up on its own feet and to develop in accordance with its own ethos."[25] Yet until 1945 nothing was done to realize this objective. The depression of the 1930s which slashed government revenue by almost 50 percent rendered the chances of investment in the South still more remote. In Khartoum, Symes's policy of "care and maintenance and his administrative measures were another blow to Southern economic development. Amalgamation of the Bahr al-Ghazal and Mongalla provinces was especially aimed at reduction of administrative work to the minimum possible. The provincial budget for 1935 was projected at E£27,388 and in 1934 the revenue of the Bahr al-Ghazal was only E£15,100. Ingelson was convinced that administrative reorganization and staff reduction would reduce the 1934 deficit from E£17,500 to E£9,657. But as it turned out, reorganization saved only E£2,795, and the difference was made up by an increase in the poll tax and by attaching the Zande district to Mongalla, thereby eliminating its charges from the Bahr al-Ghazal.[26] Administrative reorganization became the order of the day and regarded as a convenient alternative to economic development. Yet the reduction of the already small staff meant further neglect for the remote Western District.

Theoretically, the government divided the South into two economic zones: a northern Nilotic pastoralist region which included the Bahr al-Ghazal and a southern agricultural region, composed almost exclusively of non-Nilotic people.[27] In the former zone, the government saw little scope for economic development except for the simplest. "The administrative outlook with these

---

[25]F.O. 407/217, Symes to Lampson, 3 July 1934.

[26]Collins, *Shadows in the Grass*, p. 255.

[27]Raphael Koba Badal, *The origin of the underdevelopment of the Southern Sudan: British administrative neglect*, Development Studies and Research Center (Khartoum: Khartoum University, 1983), p. 16.

pastoral folks," wrote the governor general, "is strongly tinged with tribalism and essentially paternal; it aims at the condition of tribal units, compact, economically self-contained and uncontaminated by foreign contacts."[28] On the other hand, the southern Bahr al-Ghazal and Mongalla provinces presented a better opportunity for investment. There was a demand for cash, land was fertile, and road communication was better. Government intervention in this region was more conspicuous particularly in the promotion of cash crops such as cotton. The unfortunate Western District fell within the "fossilized" zone which was kept as a human "zoo." Agriculture was the vital foundation of life in the district, but production could hardly meet the bare requirements of subsistence. When crops failed or were destroyed by locusts, people fell back on wild food, fishing, and hunting. There was a chronic shortage of grain which was constantly imported from the North. The only products that could cheaply be exported were chillies, beeswax, and sesame—a local food crop with a high protein content which also enjoyed an international market as vegetable oil. However, the prices for local products were inadequate to encourage their production on a large scale. The only product in the district that the government was interested in was timber. Timber's contribution to the Forest Department was E£2,267 in 1929; E£2,191 in 1930; and E£1,398 in 1931.[29] Ivory constituted a major source of revenue in the past but by the late 1930s its supply was diminishing.

The traditional methods of cultivation and honey collection had adverse ecological effects. Land was cleared by fire which destroyed forests. Fish was killed by poison in enormous quantities. There was a great deal of musing by the Forest and Veterinary Departments officials about the introduction of new methods of conservation. These included application of the South American methods of preparing manoic, creation of natural hives without destroying trees. But these half-hearted attempts never

<hr>

[28]Raphael Koba Badal, *The origin of the underdevelopment of the Southern Sudan: British administrative neglect*, Development Studies and Research Center (Khartoum: Khartoum University, 1983), p. 16.

[29]N.R.O. Bahr al-Ghazal Province, 1/2/11, Ingelson Report on the Bahr al-Ghazal, 1935.

materialized. The government passed several laws to restrict game hunting specially by the Baqqara and the Mandala.

The one area of southern economic life in which the government intervened forcefully was trade, and retail trade in particular. Unfulfilled hopes also attended the creation of local traders to replace the jallaba. As mentioned earlier, the greatest official animus was reserved for northern Sudanese traders. Their sudden expulsion in 1930 and severance of entrepreneurial links with the North had seriously depressive effects on the southern economy. British authorities gave preference to "respectable" traders, meaning those with adequate capital and preferably non-Sudanese. Greek and Syrian traders who had come to the South after 1898 answered these requirements, but they were very thin on the ground and they were not willing to venture outside small towns. There were only three Greek merchants in Raga: Tsamouras, an agent of Lagoutaris of Wau; and Panniots and Photis who were agents of Paputside of Wau. It is true that northern traders were less capitalized than foreign merchants, they carried a limited range of goods, and so consequently charged higher prices and could not respond more flexibly to consumer demands. Moreover, government attempts to control prices were defeated by the Khartoum wholesalers. To justify increase in prices, local retailers had to bring wholesale invoices to show overcharging in Khartoum. However, the retailers were unwilling to reveal these invoices as the Khartoum wholesalers would cut their supplies. Nonetheless, the jallaba were prepared to set up their shops anywhere in the South and their substituion remained a daunting problem for British officials.

Another crippling handicap was the paucity of infrastructure in the district. With the exception of few bridges, there was no progress on the Wau-Raga road. The combination of these multiple problems meant the prospects for economic development in this remote area more bleak. All that was left to generate revenue was the collection of poll tax and tribute. Between 1929 and 1931 the ushur was raised to twenty-five piastres. Following the population movement and the depression, it was reduced to ten piastres. In 1939 tribute was raised again to twenty piastres. The locals simply had no means of earning cash to meet this burden and their response was to migrate to Darfur and other places in the north. The government had no alternative but to reduce it again to ten piasters in 1941.[30] The poll tax remained the major source of revenue in the Western District. The following table gives a clear illustration.[31]

Table 2

WESTERN DISTRICT CASH RECEIPTS:
1929-34 (in Egyptian pounds)

Year	Raga	Kafia Kingi	Total Cash Receipts	Poll tax
1929	1,378	800	2,178	1,780
1930	797	351	1,148	697
1931	848	17	865	665
1932	912	—	912	756
1933	338	—	338	179
1934	420	—	420	269

It is quite obvious that the destruction of Kafia Kingi and expulsion of its people had reduced the number of taxpayers and deprived officials of a major source of revenue.

Tax collection remained a serious problem in the Western District. There was a continuous disparity between official assessment and actual collection. In 1935 tribute was assessed at E£540, but only E£270 was collected. Moreover, the revenue that was generated from taxation went largely to sustenance of the indirect rule bureaucracy which included local chiefs and government employees. Since most people could not afford them, labor in lieu of tribute became the standard practice.

---

[30]SAD 710/10, Western District Annual Report, 1940-41.

[31]N.R.O. Bahr al-Ghazal Province, 1/2/11, Ingelson Report on the Bahr al-Ghazal, 1935.

A continuous and stable labor supply remained a problem for the colonial state. The reason is that the British were not willing to pay unskilled laborers at a suffciently attractive rate. The rate of pay for unskilled labor in the district was not increased until the late 1930s when it was raised to 1.5 piastres a day. The type of work available had not changed. Laborers were needed in the Forest Department, the sawmills, road building, and porterage. During the war years the army became one of the few venues for wage-earning employment, and a significant number of local people joined the Equatorial Corps. While the British were far less culpable than the French in regard to forced labor, nonetheless they used unfree labor in the production of essential war supplies. Since the "primitive African has in general only the work of his hands to offer" the Forest Department was able to use 25,000 men-months in their camps in the Western and the Tonj districts.

The transition to a wage-earning economy was further foiled by official antipathy. Introduction of a money economy was perceived as an element of social disruption which would lead to "detribalizaion." The situation in the Rand, in the Rhodesian copper belt and in French Equatorial Africa, were taken as warning signs of the implications of a cash economy. In the eyes of British officials introduction of money would lead to economic individualism which "while appearing to favor the native, brings him no real benefit; he may have acquired a measure of comfort, but on the other hand, the real meaning of life is lost to him."[32] In brief, the colonial economy offered very little to the people of the western Bahr al-Ghazal. The youth found no alternative but to migrate to the north. The Kreish for instance were very popular recruits in the Sudan Defence Force. British officials were disturbed by appearance in al-Fashir, al-Ubayyid, and Khartoum of skilled workers from the Western District.

In the area of health and other social services, the record was dismal. There was only one hospital in Wau, and dispensaries in Raga, Daim Zubair, Kuru, Boro, and Sopo. A patient from the rural areas did not stand much chance of survival on the rough journey to Wau. Moreover, after the reorganization of Wau,

---

[32]SAD 710/10, Western District Annual Report, 1940-41.

100

province officials were unwilling to tolerate the appearance of the rural folks in town. It was decided that "certain treatment now involving the bringing of unsophisticated people (particularly from Dinka areas) into the hospital in Wau, could, it was agreed, as well (and more economically) be carried out in the small hospitals in tribal areas of the type existing in Aweil and Raga."[33] But the two hospitals refered to had no doctor and had to depend on the annual visits of a doctor from Wau. In the late 1930s the province authorities contemplated building small hospitals in rural areas but this never materialized. Endemic diseases such as leprosy, fly blindness, and bilharzia were rampant especially around Raga. Their spread was further accentuated by concentration of people in one area after 1930. The impact of this movement was expressed by an old man to Santandrea: "Since we came here, death has been thinning our ranks as it never did in the past and seems as if it will never stop."[34] Disease and famines had taken a great toll. Their effects on the demography of the district can be illustrated by the following table.

Table 3

WESTERN DISTRICT POPULATION

Ethnic Group	1927	1946	1952
Feroge	?	832	629
Nyagulgule	689	219	171
Kreish-Hufra	?	632	627
Kreish-Naka	?	746	569
Kreish-Ndogo	?	405	365
Aja	320	167	58
Binga	370	206	234
Kara	250	80	89
Yulu	212	234	301

[33]SAD 710/10, Western District Annual Report, 1940-41.

[34]Santandrea, *Tribal History*, p. 323.

These figures were taken from tax lists which were far from accurate. Moreover, the size of the population in the district was affected by migration and other factors. Yet there is no question that the Western District has one of the highest mortality rates in the South.

If the nineteenth century was a period of violence and destruction in the western Bahr al-Ghazal, the twentieth century was a time of stagnation and destitution.

Chapter 6

EDUCATION, LANGUAGE, AND RELIGION
IN THE WESTERN BAHR AL-GHAZAL

Formal education in the southern Sudan developed within the general framework of government policy in the region and was dictated by economic and political exigencies of the time. During the first two decades of this century the British in the southern Sudan were very much concerned with the questions of security and the consolidation of their power in the region. Education, therefore, was not a compelling priority. Nonetheless, the government needed a limited number of clerks and artisans to meet the bare requirements of the administration. Thus, the seemingly convenient solution was to leave education to the Christian missions who were determined to preach the Gospel among the southern Sudanese.

For several political and economic reasons, from the very beginning education in the southern provinces was left in the hands of Christian missions. There was a traditional fear on the part of British officials that Islam would creep into their Central African territories. This fear stemmed from their experience with the Mahdi and was invigorated by numerous religious uprisings in the North during the first two decades of British rule. The potential threat of an Islamic rebellion became a nightmare for condominium officials, particularly Wingate, who was determined to keep the South "uncontaminated."

British officials, ever-apprehensive of the potential threat of Muslim "fanaticism" in the North, decided to limit the missions' activities to those areas described as "pagan," which included the South and the Nuba Mountains. From the government's perspective, Christian proselytization would find a fertile soil in the animist South, form a bulwark against Islam, and most important provide schools and teachers at no cost. This economic consideration was also of crucial importance since the government was not prepared to spend money on that aspect of southern administration.

Following the establishment of condominium rule, petitions came from the Roman Catholic Verona Fathers, the Anglican Church Missionary Society, and the American Presbyterian Church. The southern provinces were opened to these three mission groups. To avoid competition and sectarian rivalries, the South was divided into spheres of activity among the three mission groups and accordingly most of the Bahr al-Ghazal province came under the orbit of the Roman Catholic Verona Fathers of Italy. They were the largest group of missionaries and were mostly Italian, although many of the older members were of Austrian or Tyrolean origin.[1] They numbered from 150 to 300 priests throughout the period 1928-1946. The Verona Fathers were overseen by a bishop who was responsible to the Apostolic Delegate based in Nairobi and also to the headquarters in Verona.

On 12 January 1904 a group of Italian Catholic priests left Khartoum for the Bahr al-Ghazal. Headed by Francis Xavier Geyer, the group included Fathers Carlo Tappi, Stefan Vokenhuber, Antonio Viganto, Giovanni Giori, Augustus Dardelman, Clement Schoer, and Father Ohrwalder.[2] They arrived

---

[1]The latter had been much larger groups but their number had been reduced during the First World War and the balance had shifted toward the Italians who were often described as being drawn mainly from the peasants and artisan sectors of rural northern Italy. L. Sanderson, "Educational Development in the Southern Sudan, 1900-1948," *Sudan Notes and Records* 43 (1962): 105-17.

[2]Franz Xavier Geyer (1860-1943) was a Roman Catholic priest who studied at the University of Munich and the Verona Missionary Institute. He was ordained a priest in 1882 and a year later he went to the Sudan. He served in Egypt, Wadi Halfa, and Sawakin. The presence of the Roman Catholics in the South dates back to the 1840s when they founded a mission station at Gondokoro which was closed in 1863 for

at Wau on the 15th of February. To their disappointment Wau appeared to be one of the most unpromising places for missionary work. Over several decades northern Sudanese traders, soldiers, and administrators as well as West Africans had come to reside in Wau. Upon their arrival Bishop Geyer wrote: "Wau is unsuitable for a mission station at this time. I wanted a location with a heathen population, a healthy situation, and easily reached from Wau." Hence, upon the advice of Boulnois, the governor, the missionaries chose their first site among the animist population of Kayango to the northwest of Wau.[3]

In the early years of the condominium, Wingate proposed a plan for education in the Bahr al-Ghazal. According to that plan education in the province should concentrate on producing two types of employees: first, a class of fully literate military and civilian clerks, cashiers, and store-keepers; second, a group of trained artisans, carpenters, blacksmiths and other craftsmen. The first group was to be recruited from the children of northern officers, soldiers, employees, and merchants residing in Wau who would be educated in the regimental school of the battalion quartered in the town. The second group would be drawn from the local boys already serving as apprentices in government workshops.

In 1903 the Wau school was opened. The local people showed very little interest in the mission's education. It was only after chiefs and sultans were induced by officials that children became available for the school.[4] For some time the school was dominated by refugees from French Equatorial Africa and those displaced by the slave trade and the Mahdiyyah. Wingate was very much concerned with the fact that a school in a place like Wau

---

health reasons.

[3]Franz Xavier Geyer, *Durch Sand, Sumpf, und Wald* (Freiburg im Breisgau: 1914), p. 92. David Joseph Sconyers, *British Policy and Mission Education in the Southern Sudan, 1928-1946* (Ph.D. dissertation, University of Pennsylvania, 1978), p. 111; *The Golden Jubilee of Bahr al-Ghazal* (Rome: Nigrizia Press, 1956).

[4]Geyer, *Durch Sand*, p. 192.

undoubtedly would be dominated by Muslims and Arabic-speaking elements. As it turned out, of the twenty-nine boys in the school, fourteen spoke Arabic as their mother tongue, the remainder spoke a pidgin form of it and the teacher was an Arabic speaker. Thus, the secular school at Wau was handed over to the mission. There was also a fear that a northern-style *kuttab* with a Muslim teacher, even if it was secular in theory, would be an Islamizing agency in practice. Wingate promised that the education of Muslim children would be taken care of by a regimental school that would be established in Wau. In the meantime he urged Muslim parents to send their children to the technical school where they would be exempted from religious instruction.

The extension of formal education to the western Bahr al-Ghazal, therefore, was determined by these considerations and added a new dimension to the district's complex reality. The district had always been regarded by British officials as a Muslim enclave in the non-Muslim South. As mentioned previously Islamization in this part of the South was a by-product of its integration into the trans-Saharan trading network, the political and commercial expansion of Darfur and Wadai, and most important the establishment of the zariba system in the second half of the nineteenth century. Yet, the process of Islamization in this region corresponded to similar trends elsewhere in Africa. Islam was systematically adopted by the ruling families but remained superficial among the vast majority of their people. This was clearly the case with the Feroge, Nyagulgule, Kreish, Binga, Kara, and Yulu. The only form of education which existed in the district was the khalawi system in which the Quran was taught by the Borno and other West African fakis. They were scattered in different parts of the region in places like Raga, Kafia Kingi, Kabaluzu, and Gossinga. But the anticipated benefits of formal education as a means of social mobility induced some local leaders to demand a government school. As early as 1906 they had petitioned fruitlessly for a secular school, complaining that the local Khalawi catered for young boys only. When they repeated their demands again in 1910, they were told to send their children to Wau. This was the reason behind a number of boys from the

Western District in Wau school.[5] A suggestion made by the province governor to establish a government school with Christian and Muslim religious instruction as an optional extra did not materialize. However, from the very beginning the Verona Fathers were very much interested in the western Bahr al-Ghazal.

Early in 1905, Bishop Geyer toured the area with a group of other missionaries to explore the possibility of missionary work.[6] They visited Daim al-Zubair, Raga, and Gossinga. From that early encounter the missionaries showed a great deal of interest in the non-Muslim people such as the Kreish and Banda. Bishop Geyer was impressed with the Kreish, describing them as "the most religious people." Although he found some aspects of their religion repulsive, yet he regarded them as "a starting point."[7] The interest appeared to be mutual particularly among those Kreish and Banda sections who had fled from the oppressive rule of the French and the slave raids of al-Sanusi. Their sultans welcomed the idea of a mission school. Thus, from that early encounter the Kreish and the Banda offered great hope and potential for missionary work. Yet Daim al-Zubair was regarded as too sensitive an area in view of its location on the southern fringe of the Islamized groups in the district. Moreover, the Fathers themselves were discouraged by the long distance from Wau and the poor transportation system.

Thus formal education in the Western District had to wait until the mid 1920s. The missionaries did not have any hope in Raga as the "Mohammedan character of the town will endure and this would make it unsuitable for a mission." The first mission school to be established in that part of the Bahr al-Ghazal province was opened at Daim al-Zubair on 25 March 1926 by Fathers Giacomo Gubert and Luigi Bernhardt. This area was

---

[5]L. Sanderson and G.N. Sanderson, *Education, Religion, and Politics in Southern Sudan, 1899-1964* (London: Ithaca Press, 1981), p. 66. Those included the children of Said Baldas, Naser Andel, and Musa Hamid (Geyer, *Durch Sand*, pp. 230-33).

[6]They received the support and sympathy of Comyn, the first Inspector of the Western District, who was a Catholic Scot.

[7]Geyer, *Durch Sand*, p. 233.

inhabited by the Belanda, Ndogo, a few Azande, and the Kreish-Ndogo. Initially the majority of the pupils came from displaced elements such as ex-slaves, immigrants, and retired soldiers. But after a great deal of persuasion local people were gradually drawn in.[8] Hence, the first people in the district to benefit from modern education were the Belanda and Ndogo.

In brief, the system of education that was developed in the South over the years revolved around elementary vernacular schools which were erected at every mission post. At the bottom of the hierarchy and radiating from the elementary vernacular were sub-grade schools known as village or "bush schools" built in villages with the permission of the district commissioner when both the mission involved and the village chief agreed upon its desirability. Instruction was conducted in vernaculars by teachers recruited locally who had been trained in mission schools and who usually had no more than a rudimentary knowledge of reading, writing, and arithmetic. When deemed ready by the missionaries, some of the "bush school" pupils were promoted to the nearest elementary vernacular school. The first syllabus to be officially prescribed for use in the elementary vernacular was borrowed from Uganda. It included reading, writing, arithmetic, hygiene, geography, history, and physical training. Arts subjects, agriculture, and handwork were also introduced. The elementary vernacular offered a four-year course to prepare boys for work as sub-grade instructors, village medical orderlies, and chiefs' court clerks. At the highest level in the system were the intermediate schools which provided six years of work in English to supply the government with junior administrative and mostly clerical staff.

As mentioned previously, during the first two decades of condominium rule, the government did not participate directly in education in the South. It was only in the mid 1920s that it began to get involved in that aspect of life in the South. Those were the years when native administration was introduced and there was a growing need for educated Southerners to serve in the chiefs'

---

[8]The Muslim people used to hide their children from the missions and find all kinds of excuses to avoid sending them to their schools. Interview with Ibrahim Musa Ali and 'Ida Dahab, 25 July 1987.

courts and fill other clerical jobs. Moreover, the government's position became more secure and the local population began to take interest in education. The regime's intervention was also prompted by the perceived "deficiencies" in mission education. Missionary education in general and the Verona Fathers in particular came under heavy criticism from British officials. It was argued that missionary education was characterized by the lack of coherence and the absence of a unified system. The fifteen stations in the South were managed by three separate missions with varying techniques, skills, and facilities. In an attempt to ameliorate these "deficiencies," the government began to take practical steps to have some control over missionary education by providing them with subsidies in the form of grants-in-aid. This was coupled with the Non-Government School Ordinance in 1927 which required registration of all teachers in non-government schools, and that no teacher other than a native of the Sudan could be appointed to such a school without the permission of the director of education. The ordinance gave the government greater control not only over mission education in the South but most important over "undesirable" Egyptian teachers who were dominant in the *Ahliyyah* schools in the North.

The decade of the twenties was marked by a relative expansion in education in the South and new stations were opened in the Bahr al-Ghazal. Perhaps one of the most important developments was the establishment of the Lee Stack Memorial School in Wau. Its teachers were Copts and Lebanese Christians who were found and paid by the education department. Unwilling to live in the South, these teachers did not stay very long. Following a suggestion from Bishop Stoppani the government began to send a few selected pupils to Khartoum to learn Arabic and then return to teach it in the school. The first batch included Stanislaus Abdallah Peysama, Louis Dafallah Musa, and Samuel Hamad Ibrahim. A second group followed after three years.[9] Arabic

---

[9]It is said that Stanislaus was of Fur origin. He was kidnapped by the slave traders when he was a little boy, but managed to escape to Wau. He was one of the few children who went to mission schools but remained Muslim. Stefano Santandrea, "Catholic education, language,

continued to be taught in the higher classes. However, the question of language in the South remained unsettled until the Rejaf conference and the announcement of the Southern Policy. At the same time the Verona Fathers opened new stations in the province, including the one at Daim al-Zubair. The number of pupils in their elementary schools rose from 400 to nearly 1,400 during the period 1925-1930. However, this situation dramatically changed in the next decade.

For the most part, the Southern Policy was a cultural program in which education was greatly emphasized. Education was the most crucial aspect of that policy and a key to the cultural orientation of the region. The rapid expansion which characterized the previous decade was abruptly halted and even reversed as a result of the depression and Symes's policy of care and maintenance. During the period 1932-1938, there was no expansion and the enrollment in intermediate schools in particular shrank by about 12 percent.[10] This certainly was inconsistent with the stated aims of the Southern Policy. The slow progress of education during this phase may be attributed to several factors, including the general decline in the country's revenue and Symes's policy of "care and maintenance." But the real problem of Southern education lay in the absence of economic development or an expansion in bureaucracy that could absorb school-leavers.

In an attempt to buttress the Southern Policy in the Western District, Brock invited the Verona Fathers to establish a station and school at Raga. On 5 January 1932 Fathers Innocenzo Simoni and Giuseppe Pagliani set up their station at Ringi Hills only to find that the site was not suitable in this predominantly Muslim area and hence the station was closed. Raga was the seat of the Feroge and their subjects and the mission could hardly consider it a promising place. It was only in February 1935, after the population reshuffle, that the station reopened on the left bank of the Raga River.

---

and religion in the Western Bahr al-Ghazal, Southern Sudan, 1905-1956," *TransAfrican Journal of History* 9/1 (1980): 101.

[10]Sanderson and Sanderson, *Education, Religion, and Politics*, p. 171.

Expectedly, the mission's activities and education in the Western District were met by vocal protest from the Muslim communities, especially Isa Fartak. Despite the fact that two of his brothers–Tamim and Ashura–went to mission schools, Isa demanded an Arabic school for Feroge children. He relentlessly petitioned the district authorities for a kuttab in which Feroge children should be taught Arabic and Islamic subjects. The sultan's demand was ignored and he was told that he could keep two Borno fakis to run the khalawi of Raga. But Isa would not settle for less than a kuttab in his new residence at Khor Shammam. By the mid 1930s the confrontation between the Feroge sultan and the colonial government reached a peak and finally led to his dismissal. Isa tried to arouse support in the northern Sudan and Egypt. His opposition was portrayed as religious persecution and an attempt by the government to impose Christianity on a Muslim community. It was only then that British officials were alarmed. In 1937 Isa contacted Muhammad Abd al-Rahim, the editor of *Al-Nil*, and urged him to raise the issue with religious leaders such as Sayyid Ali al-Mirghani and the Shaikh al-Azhar in Egypt.[11] The matter was taken seriously by Khartoum because it could "stir up strife on religious and semi-religious grounds, which is exceedingly undesirable."[12] The civil secretary moved quickly to assure concerned circles in Khartoum that Isa's allegations were far from valid.

The question of mission education in the South in general had already been developing into a public political issue; it now became a dominant subject in the Egyptian and northern Sudanese press. Isa's dismissal coincided with intense agitation in the Egyptian press, particularly among religious circles of al-Azhar against the "suspected" Christian monopoly in the southern Sudan. In a letter from the Shaikh al-Azhar to the Egyptian prime minister, the question of Muslim revenue being expended for

---

[11]N.R.O. Bahr al-Ghazal Province 1/3/17, Isa Fartak to Muhammad Abd al-Rahim, 15 February 1937.

[12]N.R.O. Bahr al-Ghazal Province, 1/3/17, statement by Sir Stewart Symes, 2 March 1937.

Christian education was raised. London urged Khartoum to settle the issue "tactfully." After negotiations the Shaikh was allowed to propose an Islamic mission to the South with Egyptian financing as a means of easing the public pressure from Egypt.[13] Secretly, the shaikh agreed that he would not push the issue but let it die.

Isa was replaced by his brother Tamim Fartak, a medical assistant who went to the mission school in Raga. The new Feroge sultan was no less compromising than his brother and made every possible effort to prevent the conversion of his subjects such as Indiri and Kaligi. At his request the mission center established among the Indiri was closed. At the same time the Feroge children were sent to the mission school with the understanding that they would live in a boarding-house and be exempted from Bible instruction.[14]

Education could not be separated from the question of language and indeed neither could be detached from the politics of administration. Language in the South had been a problem for years with dozens of local languages and dialects rendering government education extremely difficult. For reasons that have been touched upon in earlier chapters and have been sufficiently addressed elsewhere Arabic was discouraged in South. Southern children were to be instructed in local vernaculars especially at the village and elementary levels and in English at the intermediate level. In addition to the fact that the use of vernaculars was perceived as the most logical solution, it also served a purpose for the missions. It was only through the vernaculars that they could spread their faith among the locals. The importance of vernaculars was depicted early by Bishop Geyer when he visited the Kreish in 1905. He wrote as follows:

> The one thing that stands in the way of the spreading of Islam is the negro's ignorance of Arabic. Mission schools which would teach Christianity in the native

---

[13]Sconyers, *British Policy and Mission Education*, p. 48.

[14]N.R.O. Bahr al-Ghazal Province, 1/3/17, D.C. Western District to Governor Bahr al-Ghazal, 3 February 1937.

language, teach the language itself and bring it into the realm of literature, and–for especially chosen youth–replace Arabic with English, are the means to save these heathen Kreish, who live at this border between Islam and Christianity.[15]

The most important landmark in the government's language policy in the South was the Rejaf Language Conference which was held in 1928 to deal with the question of language in the South. The conference had four objectives: first, to draw up a classified list of languages and dialects spoken in the South; to make recommendations as to whether a system of group languages should be adopted for educational purposes, and if so what languages would be selected as the group languages for the various areas; to consider and report on the adoption of a unified system of orthography; and to make proposals for co-operation in the production of text and grammar books. The conference resolved that English was to be used in government offices as well as in the intermediate and technical schools. Otherwise education should be based on the vernaculars, particularly in all village and primary schools. The conference recommended that in the future the Bahr al-Ghazal province would be served by two group languages: Dinka and Zande.[16] The latter was chosen as a group language in the Western District. The imposition of Zande was opposed by the missionaries who had been using Ndogo as a medium of instruction since their arrival in the province at Kyango and later at Daim al-Zubair school. Ndogo is the language spoken by the Ndogo ethnic group. The missionaries felt that Ndogo would be easy to spread and could give one common language to the inhabitants of the Western as well the Central Districts since many people such as the Kreish, Ndogo, some Banda, Belanda-

---

[15]Geyer, *Durch Sand*, p. 232.

[16]N.R.O. Upper Hile Provice, 1/5/131, Rejaf Language Conference 1928, Report of the proceedings.

Bviri, and the Bai could handle it.[17] In his memorandum of 1930, MacMichael had insisted that English should be used where "communication in local vernaculars is impossible," especially in the case of heterogeneous groups such as the army and the police. Every "effort should be made to make English the means of instruction among the men themselves, to the complete exclusion of Arabic."

Following application of the new policy in the western Bahr al-Ghazal, Kapala (the Kreish language) was chosen as a group language in the district after 1930. This was part of the attempt to promote the Kreish as the leading political and cultural group in the district. Again the mission favored the use of Ndogo. From their viewpoint, Ndogo was the easiest language to spread, and since it has been in use at Daim al-Zubair school it could obviate the difficulty of printing new text books. Moreover, Ndogo could also be used as a common language for the Eastern and Central districts of the Bahr al-Ghazal. Their arguments were temporarily rejected and Kapala continued to be used. However, in 1939 Ndogo was finally accepted by the colonial administration as the language of instruction in the elementary and vernacular schools, with English at the higher levels.[18] The problem of the lingua franca and the question of vernaculars is of course still a matter of debate and an issue of great political importance in present-day Sudanese politics.

Another problem of education in the South devolved from the particular character of the educational agency, being exclusively Italians operating in a British domain. Unwilling to

---

[17]According to a recent language survey conducted at Daim al-Zubair, Ndogo still has a significant presence in the area. About 44 percent of pupils interviewed spoke Ndogo with competence and 60 percent claimed some knowledge of it. Sara Yusuf Ismail and Ushari Ahmad Mahmud, *Language Survey of the Sudan, No. 1*, Institute of African & Asian Studies (Khartoum: University of Khartoum, 1978).

[18]N.R.O. Bahr al-Ghazal Province, 1/3/18, "Summary of Proposals put forward by the director of education for the Reorganization of Education in the area occupied by the Verona Fathers," Roman Catholic Mission in the Southern Sudan, June 1939.

provide education themselves, British officials nonetheless continued to question the scope and quality of missionaries' efforts. The Verona Fathers were described as rather mechanical in their methods, and "unappreciative and ignorant of British ideals and British methods of dealing with the native people."[19] Other factors affected relations between the government and the Verona Fathers. The first was the changing international situation. By the mid 1930s Anglo-Italian relations had deteriorated as a result of the alignment of Rome with Berlin, the Italian occupation of Ethiopia, and the expulsion of non-Catholic missions from that country. Hence the Italian Fathers in the Sudan became politically suspect to the extent that the British Foreign Office contemplated their removal and substitution by British Catholics. Khartoum, however, was convinced that removal of the Italian Fathers from the South would lead to the domination of northern elements and the Italian Fathers were accepted as the lesser of two evils.[20]

Usually the relationship between the missionaries and British officials tended to be determined more by the personalities involved than by formal policies and statements. In the mid 1930s for instance the district commissioner of the Western District was David Bethell, who had fought in the First World War and was known for his fervent dislike of Germans and Italians. He did not hide his resentment against the presence of eight Italian fathers in his district as opposed to one or two British officers.[21] He proposed, therefore, a reduction of their two mission stations in the district to one. But the governor was convinced that their removal would adversely affect education in the district and open the way to northern influence.[22] Not only did the Italian Fathers'

---

[19]N.R.O. Civsec, Equatoria, 17/1/3, C. Williams, "Report on Education in the Southern Sudan," February 1936.

[20]Sanderson and Sanderson, *Education, Religion, and Politics*, p. 212.

[21]N.R.O. Bahr al-Ghazal Province, 1/1/24, Bethell to Governor Bahr al-Ghazal, 23 May 1934.

[22]N.R.O. Bahr al-Ghazal Province, 1/4/24, Governor to Bethell, 16 June 1934.

techniques come under attack, but also their ability to teach English was questioned. In 1936 it was suggested that all Italian missionaries should pass an English test or be sent to Britain for crash courses in English.

Thus economic stagnation, the conflict between the missions and the government, and the general lack of economic development retarded the growth of education in the South in general during the thirties. By the end of the decade major revisions and reassessments of education in the South became inevitable. The Cox Report of 1938, for instance, called for the improvement of both the quality and the quantity of education in the South. His proposals included the upgrading of bush schools and their integration into the system as schools rather than as a proselytizing centers; an emphasis on teacher training; increased Government financial support; establishment of teacher-training centers in all mission spheres; and expansion in girls' education.

In 1944 the government announced a new program that incorporated Cox's proposals. Elementary courses were to be lengthened, teacher training schools were to be established and the need for government education in the South was emphasized. The remote Western District was not affected by these reforms. As a matter of fact, the only two schools in the district (Daim al-Zubair and Raga) were merged to form one school in Raga.[23] This school did not receive a government subsidy until 1944. However, in 1946 a government school was established among the Feroge in Khor Shmam and ten years later another one was established among the Nyagulgule in Deleba.

Introduction of missionary education in the South opened new fields of controversy. Prominent among these was the question of conversion. The government wanted the missions to produce the skills needed for administration. The missions' priority on the other hand, was to spread the faith. In theory, conversion was not essential for entry into mission schools. The government agreed with this practice as long as it was not directly involved. As far as the children of the Muslim population in the Bahr al-Ghazal were concerned they were not allowed to attend religious instruction

---

[23]SAD 710/7, Western District Annual Report, 1939.

116

without the consent of their parents. Ironically, one of the first Muslim boys to be baptized in the Bahr al-Ghazal was Mustafa, the son of the Feroge sultan Musa Hamid when he was attending the Wau school, but upon his return to Raga he recanted and returned to Islam.[24] The conversion of Muslim children was quite common and is evident in the of personal names of many people from the Western District. Most people have a Christian name, a Muslim middle name, and an African last name, which reflect the cultural stratification that was taking place in this part of the Sudan. Wingate's preoccupation with the issue of security during the early years had deterred the missions from proselytizing among the Muslim population of the western Bahr al-Ghazal. In 1914 he wrote: "It is necessary that the missions should deal very tactfully in this respect to avoid any possibility of complaints which would not only cause trouble to the Government but also adversely affect the missions."[25] The Non-Government Schools Ordinance of 1927 specified that if a child's parents objected to the Bible study segment of the curriculum he could be exempted but allowed to attend the remaining classes. This rule was of great importance in the Western District. British officials argued that if baptism was carried out against the parents' will, they would be reluctant to send their children to mission schools. They recommended, therefore, that baptism could wait until the children were eighteen years old so that they would be able to decide for themselves. It was further decided that if the missions were faced with a difference

---

[24]See Damazo Dutt Majok, "British Religious and Educational Policy" in *Religion & Regionalism in the Southern Sudan* by M.O. Beshir (ed.) (Khartoum: Khartoum University Press, 1985), p. 239.

[25]N.R.O. Bahr al-Ghazal Province, 1/4/24, Wingate to Feilden, 7 March 1914. In 1939 it was reported that in Wau school there was a total of 67 Christian pupils against the 80 non-baptized ones. N.R.O. Bahr al-Ghazal Province, 1/4/22 Bishop Orler to the Governor, October 1939.

of opinion between a minor and his parents, then the matter should be resolved with the help of the native courts.[26]

The principal of building up "a series of self-contained racial or tribal units," based upon "indigenous customs, traditional usages, and beliefs," and conversion of southern children to an alien religion appeared to be incompatible. The missionaries could not reconcile much of the traditional beliefs with their own religion. Converts had to relinquish their traditional beliefs in order to enter the Christian community. Conflicts between local practices and the new faith were manifested in the arenas of marriage and divorce, traditional dances and other social customs.[27] It is on this issue of the maintenance of local traditions and cultures that some of the eccentric British officials came to odds with the missionaries. In 1930, Brock maintained that missions and specially the Verona Fathers were there: "to break the indigenous customs, traditional usage and beliefs of the natives. Anyone passing through their hands becomes detribalised."[28] The governor was very skeptical about the mission products, "they become either converts [sic] aping European or types of effendi class despising their own people."

Another area of conflict between alien and local customs was marriage and divorce. Captain Kidd in the Western District regarded Christian marriages as "equally as foreign as Islamic ones."[29] He further suggested that such marriages should be conducted by tribal law and customs. The threat of Muslim influence continued to haunt British officials who were convinced of the frailty of African societies in their charge. "I do not think,"

---

[26]N.R.O. Bahr al-Ghazal Province, 1/4/22, Martin Parr to D.C. Western District, 14 February 1940.

[27]E.C. Sevier, *The Anglo-Egyptian Condominium in the Southern Sudan, 1918-1939* (Ph.D. dissertation, Princeton, 1975), pp. 250-55.

[28]N.R.O. Bahr al-Ghazal Province, 1/2/1, Note by Brock, 13 February 1930.

[29]N.R.O. Bahr al-Ghazal Province, 1/3/17, Kidd to Brock, 17 January 1932.

wrote Evans, "the mission personnel in general have made enough efforts to break themselves from the habit of using southern Arabic terms, names, and expressions where English equivalent exist."[30]

British officials had a fairly frozen image of the "traditional" way of life. Their vision was a web of romanticization and distaste. Despite the rhetoric about the "preservation" of local traditions, colonial officials in the South often scowled at some of the local customs such as the practice of magic and witchcraft. In 1939 Chief Bandi of the Banda was dismissed for his alleged involvement in the activities of a secret society. Some groups were singled out and praised. The Kreish were described as "very intelligent and enterprising and, as things go moral."[31] As for the Banda, " they vary from the Buru Islamized 'gentlemen' to the wild and wooly Togbo cannibal–the latter being infinitely preferable to the former. They are the proper 'slave' type-hardworking and unimaginative." The adventurous and often eccentric colonial officials were not willing to tolerate even the most trivial forms of northern influence. Bethell insisted that "shirts should be made short, with a collar and opening down the front in the European fashion and not open neck as worn by the Baqqara of Darfur." In brief, traditions had to fit in a mould caste by colonial officials.

The results of missionary activity in the western Bahr al-Ghazal can be illustrated by the following figures: in 1955 it was estimated that there were 3,522 Catholics and 843 "Catechumets" in a population estimated at 50,000. The majority came from the Belanda-Bviri, Azande, Ndogo, with a few Yulu and Kreish.[32]

Robertson's statement of December 1946 signaled the beginning of a new phase in the government's policy in the South. Although it did not mean the death of the Southern Policy, the statement was an official declaration that the future of the South

---

[30]N.R.O. Bahr al-Ghazal Province, 1/2/1, Evans to Secretary of Education, 27 August 1941.

[31]N.R.O. Bahr al-Ghazal Province, Ingelson Report, 1935.

[32]*The Golden Jubilee*, pp. 36-37.

would be linked to the North. In short, a "new Southern Policy" began in 1946. Two years later, Abd al-Rahman Ali Taha became the first Sudanese Minister of Education. Like other northern Sudanese nationalists, he adopted a formula to achieve national unity which was based on cultural assimilation with its twin components of Islamization and Arabicization of the South. Colonial policies were reversed. From 1950 onward organized Islamic proselytization began in the South. The provincial capitals of the upper Nile, Equatoria, and the Bahr al-Ghazal were specifically targeted. Mosques and khalawi were constructed in an ever increasing number. The western Bahr al-Ghazal figured prominently in this new scheme. The leaders of the nominally Muslim groups were favored and backed by successive national governments. In 1948 Stanislaus Abdallah Peysama represented this area in the Legislative Assembly. Isa Fartak returned in 1957 and was reinstated as the Feroge sultan. After independence the Feroge family continued to dominate the local politics. In the early 1960s Isa Fartak became a member of the Central Council of General Abboud. In 1968 Ashura Ahmad Fartak won election as a candidate for the Democratic Unionist party and represented the district in the National Assembly. During Numeri's regime Ali Tamim Fartak won election and became a member of the People's Council. He won again in 1986, this time as a member of the National Islamic Front.[33]

---

[33]Muhammad Ibrahim Tahir, *Tarikh al-Intikhabat al-Barlamaniyah fi al-Sudan* (Khartoum: Sudan Information Bank, 1986), pp. 16, 59, 73.

CONCLUSION

The preceding chapters reveal several facts about the recent history of the western Bahr al-Ghazal. Contrary to the long-held assumption about the geographical and cultural isolation of the South, it is evident that at least some parts of the region had developed contacts with the outside world long before the travels of Salim Quptan in 1839. Moreover, it is clear that in pre-colonial times the distinction between inhabitants of the western Bahr al-Ghazal, Darfur, Wadai, and the Chari Basin was hardly clear. Geographical barriers did not hinder the movement of people or the flow of language and other cultural traits. Kinship networks extended beyond political boundaries. Although this is a significant conclusion, it is nonetheless imperative to understand the nature and the pattern of "interaction" between the people of the Sudanic belt and those of northern equatorial Africa, as well as the context in which these contacts took place.

The overview provided in the first chapter suggests that political and military development in the northern riverine regions of the Sudan in the late nineteenth century had important political and economic consequences for the societies of the Upper Nile and adjacent territories. Expansion of the capitalist economy, and dissemination of firearms and advanced technology shifted the balance of power in favor of the northern people. In addition to this technological and military superiority, ideological factors shaped the attitude of northerners toward southern people. The absence of large-scale political organization and fragmentation of some southern societies made them an easy prey for northerners.

The incorporation of southern societies into trans-Saharan and Nilotic trading networks reached a peak in the middle of the nineteenth century. Perhaps in no other part of the southern Sudan were the effects of this incorporation manifested as they were in the western Bahr al-Ghazal. This region was transformed into a bottomless reservoir of ivory and slaves. The western Bahr al-Ghazal is a classic case of social oppression, insecurity, and exploitation. The physical environment precluded growth of a viable economy and strong political institutions that could forestall external pressure. No large state ever existed in Dar Fertit and the inhabitants had always fallen prey to external aggression.

The western Bahr al-Ghazal presents a peculiar case in the process of Islamization. Indeed, Islam had reached this area long before the coming of the Khartoumers. Islam was systematically adopted by some of the ruling families but remained superficial among their subjects. It was considered a source of prestige by which they justified their authority and maintained strong links with Darfur and the North. However, it appears that Islamic proselytization was not a primary concern of the Khartoumers and the high level of violence would have precluded any large-scale conversion. Nonetheless, the prevalence of a Muslim facade and pidgin Arabic are part of the socio-economic transformation engendered by the establishment of the zariba system.

The arrival of the British in the region at the beginning of the twentieth century was just another phase of a long history of subjugation. Emerging from half a century of turmoil, the people of the western Bahr al-Ghazal were willing to accommodate the newcomers in exchange for peace and security. Undoubtedly a relative degree of peace was provided. But whether or not colonial rule brought prosperity to the inhabitants of the western Bahr al-Ghazal is questionable. It has been argued elsewhere that British interests in the South were primarily strategic: they were there to ward off other European powers and secure the sources of the Nile. The inclusion of this vast territory within their jurisdiction was to the British an unhappy result of imperial politics. Economic development was certainly not a priority on the British agenda. In other parts of the Sudan where the British saw benefits for their home economy, they did not hesitate to intervene vigorously to impose and promote railway building and the production of raw materials. But when this investment was needed for the benefit of southern people, the British remained idle. Having no economic interest in the region, the colonial regime turned the region into a laboratory for political and cultural experimentation. One of the most cynical schemes in which they engaged was the so-called Southern Policy which was justified as a brand of native administration intended to "protect" and "preserve" traditional cultures.

Two conflicting strands are discernable in the attitude of British officials in regard to traditional cultures. On the one hand, their image of the so-called "northern influences" was derived from a mixture of stereotyping, distrust, and fear and this led to massive generalizations. The jallaba from the northern Sudan, the Dajo, the Bandala, the Hausa, and the Fulani were lumped together and viewed as "agents" of Islamization. Colonial officials could not understand the pattern and nature of Islamization in these African societies in which Islam was modified to suit the local customs. The adoption of Muslim names and certain types of dress was regarded as an"erosion" of traditional cultures. Yet, these same administrators did not necessarily embrace the local cultures they were supposed to protect. They scowled at the physical appearance of local people and customs. Moreover, British officials failed to realize that the facade of Muslim influence in the region was a by-product of a deep structural socio-economic transformation and could not be reversed by mere administrative decisions. British officials were convinced of the frailty of southern cultures. The supposed northern's threat would not have occured if a vigorous program of social and economic development was initiated in the South. But the question of "helping the South to stand on its own feet" had been phrased as wishes and hopes. The Southern Policy instead kept the South as a "human zoo."

The Southern Policy was "officially" abandoned in 1946. Ten years later, the British left the country in the hands of northern Sudanese politicians. Previous policies were completely reversed. Strategies adopted by successive post-colonial governments in regard to national unity were based on assimilation with its twin components of Islamization and Arabicization. Once again, the western Bahr al-Ghazal figured prominently in the new cultural design. A large number of khalawi, mosques, and schools were established. Successive waves of private Islamic organizations flocked into the region. The Muslim groups were promoted in terms of government services and political representation. This has led to ethnic, cultural, and plitical polarization of the western Bahr al-Ghazal which was manifested during the first civil war

(1955-1972) and became more pronounced in the current conflict. While the few educated and Christian elites sympathized with and joined the ranks of the Ananya, the Muslim groups supported Khartoum. In its attempt to combat the Sudan Peoples' Liberation army, the central government has been mobilizing the Muslim groups in the district. Private militias were recruited and historical animosities between the "Fertit" and the Nilotes were fully exploited. Thus, this remote land remains a battle-ground for two contesting cultures and a pawn in the strategic designs of external powers.

APPENDICES

Appendix A

Letter from Sultan Nasir Andel to
The Inspector Western District
Dated 24 March 1917

جناب مفتش قسم غرب بحر الغزال　　رفقته وافندم

بعد السلام اعرف جنابكم جوابكم بخصوص اولاد الدنكاوي اقور
المنهوبين وصل عندي و فهمت مضمونه وان هذه الاولاد منهوبين
حقيقه في العام الماضي وبسبب نهب هذه الاولاد بند له
كليم حربو...... دا وانصرفوا الى الرزيقات وبعد ذلك المحلا ..... قسم
سارقين شارف والد وده دخلوا دار الغربات الرزيقات و
وا بعض من اهالي انسارقين قد معا شكوى الى موسى مادبوا
بيا من اولاد الدنك يسرجعوهم الى اهاليهم والمشيخ موسى
مادبوا صبط الا راضي واخرهم عندة للحكمة ان يسلمهم الى بندا
وبندله خايفين من الدنك فبعدم رجوع الاولاد توطنوا
هناك بدار الرزيقات ولمعادوا الينا وعني مابلغن ان الا ولاد
المنهوبين بيد الشيخ موسى مادبوا قهذا اماعابت بخصوص
اولاد الدينكم ولزم تحرير هذ المعلوبين جنابكم ودفتم

السلطان
ناصر اندل

١٢٢٧
٤ ربيع ثاني

TRANSLATION

24 March 1917

Inspector, Western District,

Greetings,

I would like to inform your Excellency that I have received your letter with the regard to kidnapped children of the Dinka-Agar. In fact these children were kidnapped last year by the Bandala. As a result of this all the Bandala had run away and took refuge among the Rizaiqat Arabs. The kidnappers themselves, Sharif and al-Dudah had gone to Dar Rizaiqat. Some Bandala submitted a petition to Musa Madibo, asking for the Dinka children to be returned to them. Shaikh Musa Madibo kept the children and refused to hand them over to the Bandala. The Bandala are afraid of the Dinka. Since the children have not been returned, the Bandala decided to remain in Dar Rizaiqat and have not returned to us. The kidnapped children are in the hands of Musa Madibo and that is all that I know about the Dinka children.

Sultan Nasir Andel[1]

---

[1]N.R.O. Intel., 8/2/11, Bahr al-Ghazal Intelligence Report, April 1919.

Appendix B

Letter from Sultans Musa Komondogo to the District Commissioner, Western District
dated 10 July 1930

مقدم السلطان سيسى كمند قوا

Petitioner
Sultan Musa Kamondogo.

سلطان رحم زبير

جناب مقصد قم عزي لوقعت وقت بدر ورکرابی
اقدم ان ني قیم قبانکم والی عظیم السلطنة سلم لك
عد دتقدنا زیلی

جنا کم امرتم بنقلی مد دیم نیبر یکون جیود بدزها نفعا للسلطان
سعید بنذره ولنا طلبنا لدم جنا نیم لکن مظلوما میث متبه طینه
کرویت وبندره ویرولنا هذا اقدم منه سکنا بوه المدیریه و قد وجدت تمد حمایر
مد قدیم امزت في هذا المکان ولا الیم شجباء انتقا لی مد مکان لی لد ثبات
سعید بنذرت حیث انا ولدت بهذا المکان وکذا عموجهموض ابها مد یکون سعادة
بان اکون جکا في و مستعدا لعدم از نسال الاخیره لدقوم بما جائز وادعوا
لینا کم بطول عمني حیمي ولقد الننم

مقدمه یلمع
جها سنه

۱۹۲۰/۷/۱۰

ایفنا ثبت وکربته تاکا جماعه سعید بنذرب بینة عداوة شدیده ربما
جتا عداسیم لد تمدعا فبته في لسنقبل ولهذا للعلویه

سیسى کمند قوا

129

TRANSLATION

10 July 1930

From Sultan Musa Komondogo,
Sultan of Daim al-Zubair

His Excellency, District Commissioner Western District, Raga.

I write to you with great anticipation for help. Your Excellency has ordered my transfer from Daim al-Zubair to the Boro in the neighborhood of Said Bandas. Of all the Kreish, Banda, and Yulu sultans, I am the first to reside in this province. A long time ago, I united all the salatin in this place and I do not understand the reasons for transferring me from my place to the neighborhood of Said Bandas. My ancestors were born here. I am requesting the government to allow us to remain in our place and I am prepared to perform all my duties.

> Petitioner,
> Musa Komondogo and his people

Also there is a great animosity between us and the Kreish Naka of Said Bandas. Our association with them might lead to some troubles in the future.

> Musa Komondogo[2]

---

[2]N.R.O. Bahr al-Ghazal Province, 1/3/17.

Appendix C

Petition from the Feroge Shaikhs to the Governor
of Bahr al-Ghazal Province
dated 24 October 1930

١٩٣٠/١٠/٢٤

TRANSLATION

24 October 1930

His Excellency, The Governor of the Bahr al-Ghazal Province

With all courtesy and respect we submit the following to your Excellency with great anticipation for help. Your Excellency, you ordered all the relatives who had been living among us for a long time; with whom we intermarried, to go to Darfur. The sultan himself asked the District Commissioner that if these people, particularly the Borno, must leave, then he should allow two fakis to stay to teach our children. This has been our tradition as well as our ancestors. The District Commissioner told him that this will not be allowed and so we turned to you, hoping that you will be merciful and allow the Borno to stay with us. Otherwise, we are asking the government to transfer us to Darfur province and we are prepared to commit our energy to serve the government.

Petitioners,
All the Feroge shaikhs, Raga

Signed: Khalifa Ahmad Tahir, Hasan Kara, Kasa Babusa, Ibrahim Gandu, Sabil Abu Zala, Mahdi Uthman Khdan, Mahdi Jadid.[3]

---

[3]N.R.O. Bahr al-Ghazal Province, 1/3/17.

Appendix D

**Petition from Isa Ahmad Fartak to the District
Commissioner, Western District**
dated 30 May 1931

جناب المحترم مفتش قسم غرب ايها

أقدم هذا عريضتي لجنابكم بالنظر فيه بعين الرحمة والشفقه

في شهر فبرايو ١٩٣ حضابت ىبنة وسعاده ابكبتن كيد لمبنى
انا و شيخ نورالدين محمد شيخ لبرنوا وشيخ سليمان محمد شيخ طور
وشيخ عيسى ابكر شيخ لبعلوته وكربيج عيسى شيخ المرافيت
وشيخ عبدالتام جمعه شيخ نيام نيام وأمرتوني اما انا اكون
رئيس على قبيلة فروقي نقط و شيخ سليمان محمد يكون رئيس
على باقي المشايخ المذكورين حتى هم اختلفوا ووقفوا ذلك
وفي شهر شهير ١٩٣ انت حضابت كنت بالاجازة وقلنا سعادة
الكبتن كيد وقلنا آنه جاءه جواب فعمومى من سعاده المدير
بأن جميع الامراء اساكتين بأنها يذهبون لدار فورو ياكن
بأن جواب يسمى لعد قريب فيجب عليهم عن يجوزوا انفسهم
لغاية شهر ابريل يعنى ابريل ١٩٣ يقفوا سمه لها لدارفور وهم
جوابوا سعادته بأنهم ليس لهم غيبه بالدخاب لدارفور وسعادة
قال هذا جواب سعاده مدير الخ ـ وان لبريتكم يجب عليكم لقيام
دهم قالوا نعم ان سعادة مدير لهرنا بالامر نقوم والا ليس
لنا رغبه في لذهاب حتى حضابته أتية مه الاجابة في شهر لسهير ١٩٣

133

وأمرتهم كما أمرهم سعاده آلثنتين كيد وقلت لهم انه صار شيئ
مربوط من سعاده آلحكم العام لازم يجب عليهم القيام بهذا
حتى لضبط من حتابك غايةً منازلهم ولم اعطيهم شيئ بل
اعطيت لناس آلماكن آلذين لايقدرون لذهاب
لتمن آلهادوم نظر آلمجزوم والتاري آلثلاثه وأما الناس
آلتدد ولم المعطيهم شيئ و عند ذهابي من حتابك لوارن
تصدير لاج قابلت سعاده آلنائب و سألني ما ظلومتك
فوابته بأني قاصد نزياره ولو ليس لتكوى لاءه كل
لكلوم الغني طلبت حناء المفتش لديه هو يسبب نا طبك
به و نخاطبه ليفضى · وثانياً سعادته سألني انك تريد
تقريب لتنظيم اولاد لغروق بدبانتهم قلت له نعم وحوابني
سعادته قائلاً ان الحكومه تريد جميع من نع برالفزان في
المنفض يتكلمون بالانجليزى ليس احد يتكلم بالعرب
وبيفتح مدرسه بالانجليزى فقط ولا يفتح مدرسة عرب
وجواباً سعادته باسم مدرسة انجليزى ليس لبطال واى لغة وربنا
اذا لم يكن لصالح الرسان لم يضره بل ابنا تريد العرب لتقرير لربانه
و سألني سعادته باسم لكل لغروق يعرفون العرب قلت
له بعض يعرفوه ولبقهم يعرفوه و سعادته قان ابافتح
مدرست عرب تكون معبدلتعم عرب وانجليزى · فوابت سعادته

باب الحكومة لها دخلة بخرطوم وجد منهم عرب ومنهم
سلطانه ولكن اللغة كانت عربي والحكومة فتح لهم مدرسة
عربي وتعلموا كل التعليمات الفنيه كمثل أمور ديانتهم
ولاداب الشامه و علمهم التعليم التي قبل لم يعرفوه وفتنهم
ومدنهم وأيضاً دارفور اكثرهم سلطانه والحكومة فتحت
لهم مدرسة بالعربي وين تدرك نريد الحكومة تفتح لنا
مدرسة عربي ومدرسة انجليزي العرب لأمور الديانه وانجليزي
لفضاء اخصا للحكومة فجوابي سعادته بانه يريد عمل
استثناء وعند حضور سعادة المدير اجا فطلبت منه
برجوع لي جماعتي الكريتش سعادته فضى وطلبت منه برجوع لي
المنزله بردهم فراتيت لمين مع اولاد العرب وسعادته يفضى بل
ترد لي اثنين فقراء مع برنا لمدة سنتين فقط فوانى
بأني أريد ... مقاصمت كل شيء الذي يحمله جناب المفتش
في هذه السنه اذا نطلب اي شيء هو لا يعطيني فكن

واليوم هنايك سألني انا لي اي علوم اكتبه المين وكتبت
هذا العلوم والآخر انا علوم جداً جداً لخراب مدينتي وهرد
كل الاخراب الذي هانوا تحت رياستي و اخلاص جميع كريتش لأن
هانوا تحت رياستي لاد كل المديريات والمراكز متكونين

135

من كل القبائل وان يلبس لا تطلي انه باختلاط دنا سي بيعظهم اليمن
والقبائل بينهم وحقيقة ان الحكومه تريد رد كل القبائل
الى بلادهم قاس احمد بالطرد لسطه ازرو لبنوس السطه
سعيد نيداس والسطه ادم ينفقوا ولسطه بارود نمرلابهم
الو مس كنفقوا الغرناوي قريباً لا يزيدمتهم اونخرا سنه
دهم نا يعين كنفقوا بالغرناوي ما هم من السودان لبد هذه
الا قضيه ارضيه شايو والبرى وفنقايات و ثان وكريش
ديم زبير وكرتى يقوا ....

وانا الجلوبه واولاد العرب زطوا هذه البلد مد مده يزيد
عمه خمسين وستين سنه هنى منهم ولروم هنا وهم زرعو
ولدوا

فارجو هنايتكم كل الرجاء ..وبيننا تعمر كما كانه ن لؤول
وايضاً اجوكم ١٠ تنصروا لي انا واخواتي لخاصه با لكون
لزما لازم لنا مسيد براها وكل جمعه يأتون مابئى وناس
اكبار لصلاة الجمعه وكل مس تبعاً لي سيبنون مد اول با صا
لغا يه فوسينا

وانا لست مخالف للبصر حتى ولى اقدوم هذا بل ان اريد
العدل والانصاف والحريه التامه والأمر مفوض لنا بكم اقندم
٢٠/١/٥/١٩٢١
شهاد وقلم المطمع
عيسى حمد ترتكس

136

TRANSLATION

30 May 1931

District Commissioner,
Western District, Raga

I submit this petition to your Excellency for consideration:

In February 1930 you and Captain Kidd summoned me as well as Shaikh Nur al-Din Muhammd of the Borno, Shaikh Sulayman Muhammad of the Hausa, Shaikh Isa Abbakar of the Fallata, Shaikh Karbaj Isa of the Marafit, and Shaikh Abd al-Tam Guma of the Nyam Nyam. You told me to be the sultan of the Feroge only and asked Shaikh Sulayman Muhammad to preside over the other shaikhs of the above mentioned tribes who rejected this decision. While you were on leave in September 1930, Captain Kidd summoned us and told us that he received a private letter from the Governor indicating that all immigrants living in Raga will be moved to Darfur and an official letter to this effect will shortly come. Hence, these should prepare themselves and be ready to leave in April 1931. They maintained that they have no desire of moving to Darfur. He told them that these are the governor's instructions and he warned them they must leave. They replied that if the governor wants them to move they will leave the district but against their wish. In December 1930 you returned from your leave and ordered them as Captain Kidd had done before and told them that this order was from His Excellency, the Governor-General and that they had no choice. They requested compensation for their houses but you did not give them any help. On the other hand you compensated the poor, the blind, and the disabled. When I accompanied you to Wau in February 1931 to meet the Deputy Governor, he asked me about my complaint. I told him that I did not come to Wau to complain. I came to visit and what I have to say was told to the District Commissioner in Raga. He is my boss and he can report what I told him to you. He asked me if I want two fakis to teach the Feroge children their

137

religion and I said yes. He then told me that the government wants every one in the Bahr al-Ghazal in the future to speak English, and no one should speak Arabic. He will open an English school only. I told his Excellency that opening an English school is not a bad idea. Learning of any language in this world would certainly benefit the individual. Nontheless, we want Arabic language through which our religion could be taught. He asked if all the Feroge speak Arabic. I said no; some of them speak it and others do not. He said it will be difficult to open a school in which both Arabic and English are taught. I stated that, when the Government came to Khartoum, some of the people spoke Arabic and some spoke vernacular languages. Yet the Government established Arabic schools which taught people their religion and different kinds of trades that were hitherto unknown to them. It modernized and civilized them. In Darfur, most people speak local dialects, yet the government opened Arabic schools for them. We also want an Arabic school as well as an English school. The former for religious matters and the latter for official business. He told me that he will make an exception. When the Governor came to visit Raga, I asked him to return my Kreish subjects and His Excellency refused. I then asked him to bring the Mandala to my authority because they are Fertit, not Arabs. This had also been denied. Instead he allowed me to retain two Borno Fugara for two years only. He stated that since I opposed every thing the District Commissioner has done this, year he will not consider any requests from me, and so I kept quiet.

Today you asked me that if I have any complaint, I should put it down in writing. So I am writing this petition and I am very offended by the destruction of my town, the eviction of all the immigrants and the Kreish who were under my authority. Every province and district consists of mixed tribes and different groups. No country could progress unless its people interact with each other. If the Government really wants to return every one to his place of origin, it should have ordered Sultan Azrag al-Sanusi, Sultan Said Bandas, Sultan Adam Yongu, and Sultan Barud Nimir. They came from the French Congo less than nine or ten years ago and they are not Sudanese. This land belongs to the Indiri, Shaiu, Mangayat, Shatt, Kreish-Daim al-Zubair, and Kreish Bego.

As for the jallaba and other Awlad al-Arab, they came to this country fifty or sixty years ago and intermarried with the local people.

So I am requesting your Excellency to rehabilitate our town as it used to be. I would like you to let me and my brothers to live in Raga because we have a mosque there. Every Friday, my chiefs and the old people come for Friday prayers. All my subjects will build their houses from Raga to Gossinga.

I do not write this in disobedience to your orders, but I simply want justice, fairness, and the matter referred to your Excellency.

Your obedient servant

Isa Ahmad Fartak[4]

---

[4]N.R.O. Bahr al-Ghazal Province, 1/3/17.

Appendix E
Letter from Isa Ahmad Fartak to the Governor
of Equatoria Province

dated 30 January 1937

سعاده مدير خط الاستواء . . .

بلاغه مفتش مركز يامبيو

اقدم لسعادتكم هذا التقرير لتنظروا بعين الرحمه والعداله

انه يوم ٢٩/م حضر مدير ستر كتشنر وور مركز يامبيو

اجاء من علينا نور تمام حضور وحناء المفتش

ستندرتبل وكلهم سعادته يتجزوا الذي قدمته

من قبل لكلومبو من م٢٦ الى اخر سم . وهو تلاته

شكاوى . واحد عرضها فروعنه انا وجميع تابع فروع

واتنان تقارير للمفتش . وكلها على معنى واحد

هوان نظام اكلومبو هذا لا يريد بقاء مسلمين

في هذه المركز ولا يحب انت ان يتكلم بالعربيه ولا يفتح

مدرسه بالعربيه ومن مسلمون كيفها مشتغلنا في تغير

دياناتنا لاولادنا لاصغار . وطلبت من سعادته بان

يفتح لنا مدرسه عربيه حتى يتمكن للمدير من معرفه

اصول دينه وواجباته وسننه وحبره ليتعلم اللغه

الانكليزيه لاشغل اكلومبو واوعدني سعادته بانه سبيل

ترتيب يفتح لنا مدرسه عربيه تقريبهم ومن ذلك لوقت

اسأل للمفتش يقولون لغايه لكن ما كان لردم

لخريبه لغايه يوم ١٩٢٦/١٢/٢٨ سألت هنا بالمفتش

حتى يتمثل وقال لي لتنظر محضور مفتش لامعارف

وانتظرت لغايه يوم ١٩٣٧/١/٢٩ حضاب للمفتش ستندرتبل

حضرولنا في نوسيه اكلومبو متة بعد تفليع للمجلس

وقال لي نحن لشركته انا وستندرتبل ومفتش لمعارف

اتفقنا على ان الاولاد فروق يعلمهم بيت برامي عتمر

ليقوا للدروس عند لكتبيهم ما عندا لديانه لليغه

كربتي ولعيه بالانكليزي . وسألت هنا وبوعد

سعاده لمدير الذي اوعدني لنجرب بوعد لمرام لنا

وقالي حيا به هذا نظام اكلومبو . وقلت لنابه نحن

مسلمون واذا الاولادنا ليتعلموا باللغه كربتي وانكليزى

من ابني يتمكن من معرفه دينه وهذا ينقلبوا ضب

141

بريانه لهسلام . وقال لي جنابه ان لمارحي نخبت حلظه
بتشبيره صارحاً كل لجنوب كما حصل انفاد سدبره
عديده مع قلوبه والكلومه لوتحب انشئ لعربيه
نو لجوز ولاقري القرآن ولد دعشنام بريانه لإسلام
وقنت لجنابه ما لام لهمر هللا وعن لوتقدر مخالفة
ماصر قلكومه لوحسن اضاف تنا تبيقاً لمريبه ذرفر
وقال لي جنابه الكلومه لد نقبل ا صافتك وجميع
ما حتت وصر مادار هذا لكلام لوعين جنابه لحضر
لفنسد مستر شمل تري ٧ر٦٩٨٦/٧/ر٢٧٩ لمناسبة عليض بلدن
مع ٨ر٨٩١٢٧ دعدت بكتبت وجناب لمنضر مستر
هبجر لهم جناب مستر شمل تري بالجوابر وقال لي مستر يني
داغاً انت نستفنل صدر قلكومه وقنت له انا واحدنفر
وكل طلوم طلب من جلومى كنف اكون صد جلكومه وقال
لي الكلومه ما بضيفق لمارفر انت وجميع فرقي بل اذا
انت لينفتك نفننا لملح لن ليا شم فروقي تكتب اردروق
تكو وقنت انا اصيبر ...... اضافنى وصير ننت يني
شحتً . وقال لي جنابه مستر شمل يعنن لكلومه نقبل وقم
يوم بي طلوت تاريخ فروقي و صيم لي بالدوحش نخرت
بالبرير وحسن صفيه ةأا وضيفقه جهر لمضر وانبم صدسر
وحشيته عمر وعبدالرحمن جميو قالوا نمن وشرلنا
تنفضناً بعى لكلوم واحد كما هولكم جنابك وجناب لمنس
قل لي انتر محوتش وقال لتا يخ فروقي انظروا انتم
ليلارض عيسى جمهرتراك وهم قالوا نمن ما نعرف سبب
ليغنه وما فيادرينن رقبه وقنت لجنابه مضر لمر
جنابكم ومطيعرالامر وان نظلوم فاذا هذا اشتكاوى
لكون سبيب لرفنى مورضه لشين فنظر سعادتم
كفايه والن واقى لجميع لطلبت فلكومه وما لصبى النر
طلبه من حيلوش لمسلدك ثم ترقبه الولارنا ولابر مفوض
لشعة نتهم ٠

مشس جمر فرتاك
شيخ قبيلة فروقي   ٢٠ر١ر٧٩٩١

TRANSLATION

30 January 1937

His Excellency,
The Governor Equatoria Province,
c/o District Commissioner, Western District,

I submit the following report to be considered with mercy and justice. In 1934 Mr. Ingelson, the governor, visited Raga and from there he and Mr. Bethell, the District Commissioner, visited us in Khor Shammam. I told his Excellency about the petitions I submitted since 1929. These consist of three complaints and one petition, submitted by all the Feroge Shaikhs and myself. Two reports were also submitted to the District Commissioner. They are all concerned with the fact that the Government does not want any Muslims in this district or any one who speaks Arabic and is not willing to establish an Arabic school. We are Muslims and we are concerned with the religious future of our children. I asked His Excellency to open an Arabic school so that the pupils will be able to learn the principals of their religion and then learn English for official business. His Excellency promised me that he will make arrangements to open an Arabic school in Khor Shammam. Since then I have been waiting. He told me that he is still waiting to hear from the province headquarters. On 28 December 1936 I asked Mr. Bethell and he told me to wait for the arrival of the Inspector of Education. I waited until the 19 of January, 1937 when Hibbert came to see us in Gossinga at 6 o'clock in the evening. After the meeting he informed me the three of them (himself, Mr. Bethell, and the Inspector of Education) had agreed that the Feroge children who go to the mission school at Raga will have a separate house and be exempted from religious instructions which are taught in Kreish and English languages. I then inquired about the Governor's promise. He told me that this is the

143

Government's policy. I told him that we are Muslims and if our children are taught in Kreish and English, how are they going to learn about their religion and what will be the future of our religion? His Excellency told me that all the schools in the South are under the Mission's authority. According to him the government had decided along time ago that there will be no teaching of Arabic or propagation of Islam in the South. I told His Excellency if that is the case, we are not going to oppose the government policy and it is, therefore, better for us to be attached to Darfur Province. He told me that the Government is not going to transfer me and all my subjects to Darfur. He then asked me to go and see D.C. Bethell on 27 January 1937 for the celebration of the King's Day on 28 January 1937. I went to the D.C.s office and Mr. Hartely informed Bethell about the matter. Then Mr. Bethell came out and told me that I am working against the Government. I replied that I am just an individual and all I have done was making a request, so how can I be working against the Government? He then told me that the Government will not transfer all my people to Darfur, and if I am willing to step down as a Feroge sultan I should put that down in writing and he will approve it. I then repeated my request and said that I want the government to transfer me and all my shaikhs together. He said that this will not be possible. On the 30th he summoned the Fergoe shaikhs; they were Ali Bilul, Hasan Gharib Babur, Hasan Dahiyyah Kara, Khalifa Ahmad Tahir, Itim Jadid, Hussain Umar, and Abd al-Rahman Hamad. They told him that they all agree with their sultan. His Excellency then informed me that I am under arrest and told the Feroge shaikhs to find a substitute for Isa Ahmad Fartak. They responded that they could not understand the reason for his dismissal and they do not approve of it. I told His Excellency that I acknowledge his decision but I will take the matter to the governor. Your Excellency can judge whether my complaints and petitions warrant my dismissal and imprisonment. I performed my duties satisfactorily and all I wanted was the

144

government assistance to educate our children. I refer the matter to your Excellency.

Isa Ahmad Fartak,
Head of the Feroge[5]

---

[5]N.R.O. Bahr al-Ghazal Province, 1/3/17.

Appendix F

5 February 1937

To Muhammad Effendi Abd al-Rahim,

Greetings,

As you know, my late father was the Sultan Ahmad Fartak, son of Sultan Hamad. We are of Arab origin and all our ancestors were Muslims. You know the history of the Sudan and you knew my father personally.

In 1930 the Government expelled all the Arabs of Raga to Darfur, its policy being against the presence of Muslims in the South. We asked the Government at that time to transfer us to Darfur, but our demand was refused and we were ordered to settle in Khor Shammam, between Raga and Gossinga. We requested the provincial authorities to open an Arabic school for us, but they replied that education in the southern Sudan was in the hands of the missionaries. The Government is against the propagation of Arabic and the conversion to Islam in this area. I told them that we are Feroge and Muslims and we want to be attached to Darfur, but this fell on deaf ears. They asked us to send our children to church where they are taught the Kreish dialect in the first place and then Arabic. I told them that this is unacceptable and would jeopardize the future of our religion. They refused to allow Fugara from Darfur or Umdurman to enter this area and prevented me from sending our children to al-Fashir. I was dismissed because I opposed sending out children to church and I was removed to Wau, pending further instructions. I ask you, for the sake of our religion and your friendship with my late father, to tell Shaikh al-Islam and Sayyid Ali al-Mirghani to invite me to come and live in Umdurman. Please let me know as soon as possible.

I was not dismissed for committing any offence, but because I requested the opening of an Arabic school and for the performance of religious rites. The District Commissioner announced that he does not want the Quran to be read and Arabic customs are to be banned. The celebration of the Muslim feasts [Ramadan and 'id Adha] are also prohibited.

Isa Ahmad Fartak[6]

---

[6]N.R.O. Bahr al-Ghazal Province, 1/3/17.

Appendix G

Extract from Agreement between Governor's Darfur (Dupuis) and Bahr al-Ghazal (Ingelson) at Safaha on 28 March 1935

Entry and Exist Permits:

(a)   Entry into the Western District, Bahr al-Ghazal will be permitted to inhabitants of Darfur Province for specific purposes only and will be regulated by permit.

(b)   Entry into Darfur by inhabitants of the Western District will be similarly controlled.

(c)   In both cases persons entering without permits, and permit holders who have accomplished the object of their visit, will be returned, so far as is possible when traced. Native authorities in both provinces will be instructed accordingly."[7]

---

[7]N.R.O. Bahr al-Ghazal Province, 1/1/2.

Appendix H

Extract from minutes of meeting at Kafia Kingi, February 14th 1940 between District Commissioner Western District (Brown) and District Commissioner Southern Darfur District (Wordsworth) paragraph 3 (b).

It was agreed in general to limit the contacts between the Raga and Darfur sections of the various tribes as far as possible and to endeavor to prevent inter-marriages. Binga and Kara will only be allowed to go from one district to the other on business which has been pronounced legitimate at the annual meeting between the D.C.s and the Chiefs concerned. Other Awlad al-Arab will be given written passes by the District Commissioner, which will have to be shown to the Raga Chief concerned on arrival. Other natives of Darfur going to Raga on legitimate business will be allowed to go with passes from their tribal authorities as before.[8]

---

[8]N.R.O. Bahr al-Ghazal Province, 1/1/2.

151

Appendix I

Extract from minutes of meeting at Safaha on 17 March 1940, signed by Governor of Darfur (Ingelson) and District Commissioner Western District (Evans), paragraph c. 2.

It is agreed that in order to limit contacts between Awlad al-Arab (including Binga and Kara) and Raga District permits required by these people to visit Raga District for legitimate reasons will for the present be in English and given by the District Commissioner.[9]

---

[9]N.R.O. Bahr al-Ghazal Province, 1/1/2.

Appendix J

Extract from District Commissioner Baggara's SDD 66 E 1 of 11 April 1940, paragraph 4.

On the whole I think it would be best if we imprisoned one another's people found illegally in our area, and ordered them to be deported after imprisonment. This would give them a chance to put their affairs in order before going and also would lead to future convictions. Many of those found illegally crossing the boundary seem to have criminal records.[10]

---

[10]N.R.O. Bahr al-Ghazal Province, 1/1/2.

Appendix K

Extract from District Commissioner Western District's 8 B 1 of 16 January 1941, written from Khor Shammam to District Commissioner Baqqara, paragraph 9.

Chief Tamim has been giving one or two "permits to visit friends". This quite defeats the purpose shown in para. 3 (b) of your and Major Brown's record of Kafia Kingi meeting of 14.2.40 (Note i.e. 2 above) but is not precisely forbidden thereby. I have now precisely and strongly forbidden it.[11]

---

[11]N.R.O. Bahr al-Ghazal Province, 1/1/2.

Appendix L

Extract from District Commissioner Western District's (Evans) 8 B 1 of 23 January 1941 written at Said Bandas to District Commissioner Baqqara(Wordswoth), paragraph 8.

I have found your agreement with Major Brown at Kafia Kingi on 14 February 1940 very difficult to administer as regards para 3 (b) (NOTE i.e. 2 above) owing to the distinctions there made in the treatment as regards crossing the border of the various tribes. The only way on this side to further the object shown in the first sentence of that para,i.e. *to cut contact*, is to make *all* crossing of the frontier illegal by any native of Western District without a written pass from District Commissioner, W.D. I have given out that this must be obeyed as an order from now on. So anyone going up now without a District Commissioner's pass will I hope be jailed by you as you suggest vide (i.e. Note 4 above) before return. Could you make the same order? At present Western District Chiefs will detain for investigation and send me news at once of any of your people appearing without a paper from you. Without this I do not see that visits and intermarriage will ever cease.[12]

---

[12]N.R.O. Bahr al-Ghazal Province, 1/1/2.

Appendix M

Extract from District Commissioner Baqqara's (Wordsworth) SDD 66 E 1 of 8 February 1941 to District Commissioner, WD (Evans) para. 5.

I agree with your para 8 (NOTE i.e. 6 above). I was over per-suaded about the passes. I will try again to get the ruling that English passes are needed for all movers. I may issue a few blanks to reliable "pure" Arab Nazirs for genuine Arabs, and issue passes to others ("Awlad Arab," Mandala etc) myself. Would that do? I will also instruct our chaps to arrest anyone of your chaps found here without your new order pass. I have given very few passes myself this year, and have refused hundreds.[13]

---

[13]N.R.O. Bahr al-Ghazal Province, 1/1/2.

Appendix N

Extract from minutes of meeting at Safaha on 4 March 1941, signed by District Commissioner Western District (Elliot-Smith) and District Commissioner Southern Darfur (Nightingale).

It is agreed that the existing arrangements about passes to visit Equatoria Province shall continue for the present; viz. that none of the Awlad Arab are allowed to visit the W.D. without a pass from the District Commissioner S.D. and that Arabs generally get passes from their Nazir (this does not apply to Rizaigat visiting Aweil). Any Mandala found in W.D. without a pass from his Nazir will be arrested. Anyone visiting the Bahr el-Arab from W.D. must have a pass from the D. Commissioner.[14]

---

[14]N.R.O. Bahr al-Ghazal Province, 1/1/2.

GLOSSARY

ahrar	free born men
amir	king or chief
araqi	a locally brewed liquor
asakir	soldiers
bahara	sailors
baziner	irregular soldiers
daim	neighborhood, used to denote residential quarters in Khartoum
diya	blood money
faki	religious teacher or scholar
furukh	young slaves
jallaba	peddlar
khalawi	plural of khalwa, Quranic school
kuttab	elementary school
maqdum	a high office in the Fur sultanate
mamur	district official
mulazim	companion
razzia	slave raid
shartay	a high office in the Fur sultanate
shaikh	tribal or religious leader
suq	market
ushur	one-tenth; a tithe levied on agricultural production
wakil	agent

BIBILIOGRAPHY

Oral Sources

Ibrahim Musa Ali	Yulu
'Ida Dahab	Yulu
Adam Kuvolo	Binga
Ali Duldum	Mandala
Khamis Bakhit	Kreish
Muhammad Mayama	Kreish
Barud Yandyer	Banda
Azraq Nglindi	Banda

Unpublished Documentary Sources

Archives of the Sudan Government, National Records Office, Khartoum. (N.R.O.)

The documents relating to each of the Southern provinces are kept in separate files. The principal classification researched for this study is records of Bahr al-Ghazal Province. Documents in the N.R.O. are listed by class number, box number, and file number.

Bahr al-Ghazal Province

1/1/1-2.
1/2/1-11
1/3/12-18
1/4/19-24
1/5/25-31
1/6/32-37
1/7/38-39
1/8/40-42

Civsec

> These are the files of the civil secretary which include correspondence with provinces and district officers. The following files were consulted:

> 1/3/43-44
> 1/5/11
> 35/2/5-6
> 50/57/56
> 66/2/12-13
> 103/1/1

Darfur Province

> 7/1/3
> 7/2/5-7

Intel

> These are the records of the Intelligence Department. They contain material of general administrative interest down to the early 1920s. As far as the Bahr al-Ghazal is concerned the following files are relevant.

> 2/5/20
> 2/13/112
> 2/13/155
> 2/26/208-217
> 2/43/366
> 5/4/48
> 5/5/53
> 8/1/6
> 8/2/7-11

Mahdiyyah

The most relevant material is the correspondence between Karamallah al-Kurkasawi and the Khalifa, and between al-Khatim Musa and Mahmud wad Ahmad. These letters are to be found in:

1/14/3
1/14/3/308-360

Palace

3/2/17
5/1/1
20/20/90.

The Archives of the Foreign Office, Public Record Office, London.

F.O. 141:

90, 129, 479, 490, 510, 529, 560, 630, 737, 767, 1339, 2221, 2228, 2457.

F.O.371:

246-47 659, 890, 1111, 1361, 1965, 2349.

Private Collections: Sudan Archive, Durham University, Great Britain

This is a collection of the papers of former officials, soldiers, missionaries, business men, and individuals who served during Anglo-Egyptian rule. As far as the western Bahr al-Ghazal is concerned, the most relevant are the papers of:

Evans, D.M.   : 710/7-10.
Robertson, J.   : 520-530.
Simpson, S.R.   : 720/4

In addition, the following material was consulted:

212/10/8
243/8
248/34
586/1/20

Sudan Library, University of Khartoum

This collection contains miscellaneous collections of official publications and reports. Of particular importance are the Intelligence Reports of the early years of the condominium.

School of Oriental and African Studies, University of London

The papers of Rev. Dr. A.J. Arkell, former administrator in Darfur and Commissioner of Archaeology. They comprise four boxes with the classified reference of AP.

Theses and Dissertations

Cordell, D.D. *Dar al-Kuti: A History of the Slave Trade And State Formation on the Islamic Frontier in Northern Equatorial Africa (Central African Republic and Chad) in the Nineteenth and Early Twentieth Centuries* (Ph.D., University of Wisconsin-Madison, 1977).

Hargey, T.M., *The Suppression of Slavery in the Anglo Egyptian 1899-1939* (D. Phil., Oxford, 1983).

Majok, Damazo Dut, *The Bahr al-Ghazal During the Condominium Period, 1900-1927* (M.A., Khartoum University, 1978).

Saeed, A. *The State and Socio-economic Transformation in Sudan: The Case of Social Conflict in Southern Kurdufan* (Ph.D., University of Connecticut, 1982).

Sconyers, D.J. *British Policy And Mission Education in the Southern Sudan, 1926-1946* (Ph.D., University of Pennsylvania, 1978).

Sevier, C.E. *The Anglo-Egyptian Condominium in the Southern Sudan: 1918-1939* (Ph.D., Princeton, 1975).

Published Materials

Official

Beaton, A.C. *Equatoria Province Handbook*, 2 vols., Sudan Government Publication, 1949.
The Bahr el-Ghazal Handbook, Sudan Government Publication, 1911.
Sudan Monthly Record, 1930-1948.
The Golden Jubilee of the Bahr al-Ghazal, Rome: Nigrizia Press, 1956.

Books in Arabic

al-Hasan, M.A. *Tarikh Darfur al-Siyasi*. Khartoum: Khartoum University Press, 1971.
Makki, Hasan. *al-Siyasah al-Ta'limyah wa al-Thagqafa al-Arabiyah fi Janub al-Sudan*. Khartoum: African Islamic Institute, 1983.
Maqqar, Nasim. *al-Bikbashi al-Misri Salim Quptan wa al-Kshf 'an manabi' al-Nil*. Cairo, 1960.
Shukri, M.F. *al-Hukm al-Misri fi al-Sudan*, 1820-1880. Cairo, 1947.
Tahir, Muhammad Ibrahim. *Tarikh al-Intikhabat al-Barlamaniyah fi al-Sudan*. Khartoum: Sudan Information Bank, 1986.
Toniolo, E. *Dur al-Irsaliyat al-Kathulukiyah fi Harakat al-Kashf al-Jughrafi wa 'ilm al-Ajnas al-Bahariyah bil Sudan ma bayn 1842-1899*. Khartoum, 1958.
Tusun, Umar. *Tarikh Mudiryat Khat al-Istawa' al-Misriyah min fathaha ila dayai'ha, 1869-1889*. Cairo, 1937.
al-Tunisi, Muhammad Ibn Umar. *Tashidh al-Adhhan bi Sirat bilad al-'Arab wa al-Sudan*. Cairo, 1965.
al-Zubair, Sa'd al-Din. *Al-Zubair Rajul al-Sudan*. Cairo, 1952.

Books in European Languages

Abd al-Rahim, M. *The Development of British Policy in the Southern Sudan, 1899-1947*. Khartoum: Khartoum University Press, 1968.

_____. *Imperialism and Nationalism in the Sudan*. Oxford: Oxford University Press, 1969.

Adeleys, R.A. "Rabih Fadallah, 1879-1893: Exploits and impact on Political relations in Central Sudan." *Journal of the Historical Society of Nigeria* 5/2 (1979): 223-42.

Ali, Abbas I.M. *The British, the Slave Trade, and Slavery in the Sudan*. Khartoum: Khartoum University Press, 1975.

al-Nagar, U. *The Pilgrimage Tradition in West Africa*. Khartoum: Khartoum University Press, 1972.

Allen, B.M. *Gordon and the Sudan*. London: Macmillan, 1931.

Arkell, A.J. "The History of Darfur, A.D. 1200-1700, Part 1." *Sudan Notes and Records* 32 (1951): 37-70.

Asad, T. (ed.). *Anthropology and the Colonial Ecnounter*. London: Ithaca Press, 1973.

Badal, R.K. *Origins of the Underdevelopment of the Southern Sudan: British Administrative Neglect*. Development Studies Center. Khartoum: University of Khartoum, 1983.

Baiers, S. "Trans-Saharan Trade and the Sahel: Damergn, 1870-1930." *Journal of African History* 18 (1970): 37-60.

Baker, S. *The Albert N' Yanza*. London: Macmillan, 1885.

Balamoan, G.A. *Peoples and Economies in the Sudan, 1884-1956*. Cambridge: Harvard University Press, 1976.

Barbour, K.M. "The Wadi Azum." *The Geographical Journal* 120 (1954): 172-82.

_____. *The Republic of the Sudan: A Regional Geography*. London: University of London, 1969.

Barth, F. (ed.) *Ethnic Groups and Boundaries*. London: Allen and Unwin, 1969.

Beshir, M.O. *The Southern Sudan: Background to Conflict*. Khartoum: Khartoum University Press, 1968.

Bejorkelo, A. "Turco-jallaba relations, 1821-1885." In *Trade and Traders in the Sudan*, ed. Leif O. Manger. Bergen: Bergen University Press, 1981, pp. 81-107.

Browne, W.G. *Travels in Africa, Egypt, and Syria from the year 1792 to 1798*. London: Murray, 1806.

Casati, G. *Ten Years in Equatoria and the Return with Amin Pasha*. London: Frederick Warne, 1891.

Chevalier, A. *L'Afrique Central Francaise, Recit du Vougye de al Mission*. Paris: Challamet, 1907.

Collins, Robert O. *The Southern Sudan, 1883-1898: A Struggle for Control*. New Haven: Yale University Press, 1964.

_____. "The Establishment of Christian Missions and their Rivalry in the Southern Sudan." *Tarikh* 3/1 (1969): 38-47.

_____. "Sudanese Factors in the History of the Congo and Central West Africa in the Nineteenth Century." In *Sudan in Africa*, ed. Yusuf Fadl Hassan. Khartoum: Khartoum University Press, 1972.

_____. "The Sudan Political Service: A Portrait of the Imperialist." *African Affairs* 81 (1972): 293-303.

_____. *Land Beyond the Rivers: The Southern Sudan, 1898-1918*. New Haven: Yale University Press, 1971.

_____. *Shadows in the Grass: Britain in the Southern Sudan, 1918-1956*. New Haven: Yale University Press, 1983.

Comyn, D.C.E. *Service and Sports in the Sudan; a record of administration in the Anglo-Egyptian Sudan, with some intervals of sport and travel*. London: John Lane, 1911.

Cooper, F. "The Problem of Slavery in African Studies." *Journal of African History* 20 (1979): 30-74.

Cordell, Dennis. "The Savannas of North-Central Africa." In *History of Central Africa*, vol. 1, ed. David Birmingham and Phyllis Martin. London: Longman, 1983.

_____. "The Delicate Balance of Force and Flight: The End of Slavery in Eastern Ubangi-Shari." A paper presented at the African Studies Annual Meeting, New Orleans, 1985.

Daigre, M. *Oubangui-Chari*. Paris: 1950.

Deng, F.M. *Dynamics of identification: A basis for national integration in the Sudan*. Khartoum: Khartoum University Press, 1973.

_____. *Africans of Two Worlds: The Dinka in Afro-Arab Sudan*. New Haven: Yale University Press, 1978.

Douin, G. *Histoire du Regne du Khedive Ismail: L'Empire Africain*, 3 vols. Cairo: Société Royale de Géographie d'Egypt, 1963.

El-Malouf, A. "The occupation of Bahr el-Ghazal, 1900." *Journal of the Egyptian Society of Historical Studies* 2 (1952): 136-45.

Evans Pritchard, E.E. "The Bongo." *Sudan Notes and Records* 12 (1929): 1-62.

_____. *The Azande*. Oxford: Oxford University Press, 1971.

Fisher, A.G.B. and Fisher, H.J. *Slavery and Muslim Society in Africa*. London: Hurst, 1970.

Gessi, R. *Seven Years in the Sudan*. London: Sampson, Low, Marston, 1892.

Geyer, Franz Xaver. *Durch Sand, Sumpf, und Wald: Missions reisen in Zentral Afrika*. Freiburg im Breisgau: 1914.

Gray, Richard. *A History of the Southern Sudan, 1839-1889*. London: Oxford University Press, 1961.

Greenberg, J.H. *The Languages of Africa*. Bloomington: Indiana University Press, 1966.

Haaland, Gunnar. "Economic determinant in ethnic process." In *Ethnic Groups and Boundaries*, ed. F. Barth. London: Allen and Unwin, 1969.

_____. "Ethnic groups and language use in Darfur." In *Aspects of Language in the Sudan*, ed. R. Thelwall. London: The New University of Ulster, 1978, pp. 181-99.

Hallam, W.K.R. *The Life and Times of Rabih Fadl Allah*. Devon: Arthur Stockwell, 1977.

Hassan, Y.F. (ed.). *Sudan in Africa*. Khartoum: Khartoum University Press, 1971.

Hebbert, G.K.C. "The Mandala of the Bahr el-Ghazal." *Sudan Notes and Records* 8 (1925): 187-93.

Henerson, K.D.D. *Sudan Republic*. London: Ernest Benn, 1953.

Hill, R.A. *A Biographical Dictionary of the Anglo-Egyptian Sudan*. Oxford: Oxford University Press, 1951.

_____. *Egypt in the Sudan, 1820-1881*. Oxford: Oxford University Press, 1959.

Holt, P.M. *The Mahdist State in the Sudan*. Oxford: Oxford University Press, 1958.

Ismail, S.Y. and Mahmud, U.A. *Language Survey of the Sudan*. Khartoum: Institute of African and Asian Studies, 1979.

Jackson, H.C. *Black Ivory: The Story of el-Zubair Pasha, Slaver and Sultan*. Oxford: Blackwell, 1913.

Jennings, B. "Tales of the Wadai Slave Trade in the Nineteenth Century; told by Yunes Bedis." *Sudan Notes and Records* 13 (1930).

174

Junker, W. *Travels in Africa*, 3 vols. London: Chapman and Hall, 1890.

Kalck, P. *Central African Republic*. London: Pall Mall Press, 1971.

Lugard, F.D. *The Dual Mandate in British Tropical Africa*. London: Frank Cass, 1965.

Lewis, I.M. *Islam in Tropical Africa*. London: Oxford University Press, 1966.

Mack, J. and Robertshaw, (eds.). *Culture History in the Southern Sudan*. Nairobi: East African Studies Institute, 1982.

MacMichael, H.A. *The Anglo-Egyptian Sudan*. Cambridge: Faber and Faber, 1922.

Mahmud, U.A. *Arabic in the Southern Sudan: History and Spread of a pidgin Creole*. Khartoum: FAL Advertising and Printing Co., 1983.

Majok, D.D. "British Religious And Educational Policy: The case of Bahr al-Ghazal." In *Religion & Regionalism in the Southern Sudan*, ed. Muhammad Umar Beshir. Khartoum: Khartoum University Press, 1985.

Manger, Leif O. (ed.). *Trade and Traders in the Sudan*. Bergen: University of Bergen, 1984.

Murice, G.K. "The History of Sleeping Sickness in the Sudan." *Sudan Notes and Records* 13 (1930): 211-45.

Nachtigal, G. *Sahara and the Sudan*, vol. 4. Berkely: University of California Press, 1971.

Nadler, L.F. *A Tribal Survey of Mongalla Province*. London: Negro University Press, 1973.

O'Fahey, R.S. *State And State Formation in the Eastern Sudan*. Institute of African and Asian Studies. Khartoum: University of Khartoum, 1970.

_____. "Slavery and the Slave Trade in Dar Fur." *Journal of African History* 14 (1973): 29-43.

_____. "Fur and Fartit: A History of a Frontier." In *Culture History in the Southern Sudan*, ed. John Mack and Robertshow. Nairobi: British Institute in Eastern Africa, 1983, pp. 75-87.

_____. *State and Society in Dar Fur*. New York: St. Martin's Press, 1980.

Petherick, J. *Travels in Central Africa and Explorations of the Western Nile Tributaries*, 2 vols. London: Tinsley Brothers, 1869.

Sanderson, L. and Sanderson, G.N. *Education, Religion, and Politics in Southern Sudan, 1899-1964*. London: Ithaca Press, 1981.

Santandrea, Stefano. "The Belanda, Ndogo, Bai, and Sere in the Bahr el-Ghazal." *Sudan Notes and Records* 16 (1933): 161-80.

_____. "Shilluk-Luo tribes in the Bahr al-Ghazal." *Internatioal Review of Ethnology and Linguistics* 37 (1942): 231-40.

_____. "The Little unknown tribes of the Bahr el-Ghazal." *Sudan Notes and Records* 29 (1948): 78-106.

_____. "Gleaning in the Western Bahr al-Ghazal." *Sudan Notes and Records* 31 (1950): 54-64.

_____. "Musing on the Banda." *Messenger* (April-May 1951).

_____. "A preliminary Account of the Indiri, Togoyo, Feroge, Mangaya, and Woro." *Sudan Notes and Records* 34 (1953): 257-64.

_____. "The Belgians in the Western Bahr el-Ghazal." *Sudan Notes and Records* 35 (1955): 188-97.

_____. "Sanusi, Ruler of Dar Banda and Dar kuti in the history of the Bahr el-Ghazal." *Sudan Notes and Records* 38 (1957): 151-55.

_____. *A Tribal History of the Western Bahr al-Ghazal*. Bologna: Editrice Nigrizia, 1964.

_____. *The Luo of the Bahr el-Ghazal*. Bologna: Editrice Nigrizia, 1968.

_____. *Ethno-geography of the Bahr el-Ghazal*. Bologna: Editrice Nigrizia, 1968.

_____. *A Popular History of Wau*. Rome: 1977.

_____. "Catholic Education, Language, And Religion in the Western Bahr el-Ghazal, Southern Sudan, 1905-1955." *Trans-Africa Journal of History* 9/1 (1980): 91-102.

Schweinfurth, Georg. *The Heart of Africa*. 2 vols. New York: Harper, 1873.

Shukry, M.F. *The Khedive Ismail and Slavery in the Sudan*. Cairo: Librairie La Renaissance d'Egypte, 1937.

Slatin, R.G. *Fire and Sword in the Sudan*. London: Harper, 1896.

Spaulding, Jay. "Slavery, Land Tenure, and Social Class in the Northern Turkish Sudan." *International Journal of African Historical Studies* 15 (1982): 1-20.

Taha, F.A.A. "The Boundary Between the Sudan, Chad, And The Central African Republic." *Sudan Notes and Records* 60 (1979): 1-14.

Theobold, A.B. *Ali Dinar, Last Sultan of Darfur, 1898-1916*. London: Longman, 1956.

Tosh, John. "The Economy of the Southern Sudan under the British, 1898-1955." *Journal of Imperial And Commonwealth History* 9 (May 1981): 275-88.

Tucker, A.N. "The tribal confusion around Wau." *Sudan Notes and Records* 14 (1931): 49-60.

_____. *The Eastern Sudanic Languages*. London: Dawsons of Pall Mall, 1940.

Walz, T. *Trade Between Egypt and Bilad al-Sudan*. Cairo: 1978.

Wilson, C.T. and Felkin, R.W. *Uganda and the Egyptian Sudan*, 2 vols. London: 1882.

INDEX

179

180

Gabir, 27.
Gall, 58.
Gessi, Romolo, xviii, 11.
Geyer, F.X., 27, 104, 105, 107, 112, 113, 174.
Gillan, 80, 81.
Ginawi, 3.
Golo, xii, 3, 8, 12, 13, 17, 41.
Gordon, C., 11, 16, 62, 172.
Gossinga, 23, 26, 27, 32, 83, 84, 106, 107, 139, 143, 147.
Guju, 3.

Habbaniya, 37, 40, 72.
Hakim, Bandas, 12, 14.
Hamid, Musa, 16, 23, 24, 27, 28, 48, 49, 86, 107, 117.
Hausa, xii, 1, 67, 71, 123, 137.
Hebbert, G.K., xix, 40, 56, 58, 73, 174.
Hilali, 9.
Hufrat al-Nahas, 1, 9, 10, 13, 18, 27, 36, 49.

Ibrahim, Murad, 28, 49.
Indiri, xv, 54, 76, 83, 85, 86, 88, 112, 138, 176.
Ingelson, 76, 81, 89, 90, 96, 97, 99, 119, 143, 149, 153.

Jabal Marra, xv, 78.
Jali, 35, 44-46, 78.
Jallab, 34, 46, 47, 85.
Jallaba, 1, 3, 5-7, 9, 11, 13, 15, 35, 39, 67-69, 94, 98, 123, 139, 165, 172.
Jihadiyah, 26.
Junker, W., xviii, 175.

Kabaluzu, 1, 23, 26, 32, 34, 40, 68, 76, 106.
Kafia Kingi, xx, 1, 14, 23, 26, 27, 31, 32, 34, 35, 37, 40, 43, 45, 46, 49, 50, 56, 60, 68, 70, 71, 75, 77, 78, 82, 87, 88, 90, 99, 106, 151, 157, 159.
Kaligi, xvi, 53, 86, 112.
Kamun, Abdullahi, 44, 45.
Kapala, 84, 88, 114.
Kara, xii, xiii, xiv, xv, 11, 14, 15, 20, 27, 37, 53, 54, 77-83, 89, 101, 106, 132, 144, 151, 153.
Kayango, 13, 105.
Khalifa, xix, 17, 19, 132, 144, 169.
Khandaq, 46.
Khedive, 24, 173, 176.
Kogul, 75.
Komondogo, 27, 77, 129, 130.
Kreish, xii, xiii, xiv, xv, xvi, 3, 8, 11-15, 18, 20, 27, 44, 45, 48, 49, 53, 54, 77, 78, 82-88, 100, 101, 106-108, 112-114, 119, 130, 138, 143, 144, 147, 167.
Kuchuk Ali, 3.
Kurdufan, 7, 9, 11, 30, 34, 35, 43, 65, 67, 68, 71, 170.
Kurkusawi, xix, 17.
Kuru, 26, 59, 83-85, 92, 100.

Lampen, G.D., 42, 65, 72-75.
Leopold, 18.
Luo, 57, 176.

Lupton, 17.

MacMichael, H., 61, 62, 64, 69, 70, 72, 95, 114, 175.
Macphail, J., xx, 56, 58, 59.
Madibo, Musa, 41, 128.
Mahdist, xvii, xviii, 6, 16, 17, 19, 20, 36, 48, 52, 62, 174.
Mahmud wad Ahmad, xix, 169.
Malazac, 3.
Mandala, 27, 40-42, 93, 98, 138, 161, 163, 167, 174.
Mande, E.W., 34.
Mangayat, 54, 76, 83, 85, 138.
Marshr'a al-Raqq, 23.
Marwood, B.V., 95.
Meridi, 25.
Milner, 61.
Monbuttu, xviii.
Muhammad Ali, 2, 16.

Ndele, 14, 35, 43, 45, 46, 48, 49.
Ndogo, xii, 3, 8, 11, 13, 14, 17, 27, 54, 55, 77, 84, 87, 101, 108, 113, 114, 119, 176.
Ngsanga, 85.
Nilis, 18.
Nyagulgule, xii, xiii, xiv, xv, xvi, 14-19, 21, 27, 40, 41, 48, 53-55, 68, 75, 76, 78, 83, 101, 106, 116.
Nyala, 71.

Ohrwalder, 104.
Owen, R.C., 58, 63, 95.

Parr, Martin, 81, 91, 118.
Petherick, J., 3, 176.
Peysama, S., 109, 120.
Poncet, J., 3.
Pongo, 31.

Rabih Fadl Allah, 9, 11, 174.
Radom, 73, 79.
Raga, 14, 19, 20, 23, 26, 27, 31-35, 37-40, 47, 48, 53, 56, 60, 68, 70, 71, 76, 77, 84, 86, 88-90, 92, 95, 98-101, 106, 107, 110-112, 116, 117, 130, 132, 137-139, 143, 147, 151, 153.
Razzia, 165.
Rizaiqat, 9, 16, 37, 40, 41, 128.
Robertson, J., 95, 119, 169.
Rohl, xviii.
Rowland, 75.
Runga, Dar, 37.

Safaha, 79, 80, 149, 153, 163.
Santandrea, S., xv, xx, 17, 54, 57, 78, 85, 101, 109, 176.
Sara, 12, 67, 71, 114.
Schoer, C., 104.
Schuster, 63.
Sere, xii, 17, 176.
Shaikan, 16.
Shaiu, xv, 54, 76, 83, 86, 88, 138.
Shala, xiii.
Shaka, 8, 9.
Shatt, 54, 56-59, 77, 83, 85, 88, 138.

MONOGRAPHS IN INTERNATIONAL STUDIES

ISBN Prefix 0-89680-

Africa Series

36. Fadiman, Jeffrey A. THE MOMENT OF CONQUEST: Meru, Kenya, 1907. 1979. 70pp.
    081-4 $ 5.50*

37. Wright, Donald R. ORAL TRADITIONS FROM THE GAMBIA: Volume I, Mandinka Griots. 1979. 176pp.
    083-0 $15.00*

38. Wright, Donald R. ORAL TRADITIONS FROM THE GAMBIA: Volume II, Family Elders. 1980. 200pp.
    084-9 $15.00*

41. Lindfors, Bernth. MAZUNGUMZO: Interviews with East African Writers, Publishers, Editors, and Scholars. 1981. 179pp.
    108-X $13.00*

43. Harik, Elsa M. and Donald G. Schilling. THE POLITICS OF EDUCATION IN COLONIAL ALGERIA AND KENYA. 1984. 102pp.
    117-9 $12.50*

44. Smith, Daniel R. THE INFLUENCE OF THE FABIAN COLONIAL BUREAU ON THE INDEPENDENCE MOVEMENT IN TANGANYIKA. 1985. x, 98pp.
    125-X $11.00*

45. Keto, C. Tsehloane. AMERICAN-SOUTH AFRICAN RELATIONS 1784-1980: Review and Select Bibliography. 1985. 159pp.
128-4 $11.00*

46. Burness, Don, and Mary-Lou Burness, ed. WANASEMA: Conversations with African Writers. 1985. 95pp.
129-2 $11.00*

47. Switzer, Les. MEDIA AND DEPENDENCY IN SOUTH AFRICA: A Case Study of the Press and the Ciskei "Homeland". 1985. 80pp.
130-6 $10.00*

48. Heggoy, Alf Andrew. THE FRENCH CONQUEST OF ALGIERS, 1830: An Algerian Oral Tradition. 1986. 101pp.
131-4 $11.00*

49. Hart, Ursula Kingsmill. TWO LADIES OF COLONIAL ALGERIA: The Lives and Times of Aurelie Picard and Isabelle Eberhardt. 1987. 156pp.
143-8 $11.00*

50. Voeltz, Richard A. GERMAN COLONIALISM AND THE SOUTH WEST AFRICA COMPANY, 1894-1914. 1988. 143pp.
146-2 $12.00*

51. Clayton, Anthony, and David Killingray. KHAKI AND BLUE: Military and Police in British Colonial Africa. 1989. 235pp.
147-0 $18.00*

52. Northrup, David. BEYOND THE BEND IN THE RIVER: African Labor in Eastern Zaire, 1865-1940. 1988. 195pp.
151-9 $15.00*

53. Makinde, M. Akin. AFRICAN PHILOSOPHY, CULTURE, AND TRADITIONAL MEDICINE. 1988. 175pp.
152-7 $13.00*

54. Parson, Jack, ed. SUCCESSION TO HIGH OFFICE IN BOTSWANA. Three Case Studies. 1990. 443pp.
157-8 $20.00*

55. Burness, Don. A HORSE OF WHITE CLOUDS. 1989. 193pp.
158-6 $12.00*

56. Staudinger, Paul. IN THE HEART OF THE HAUSA STATES. Tr. by Johanna Moody. 1990. 2 vols. 653pp.
160-8 $35.00*

57. Sikainga, Ahmad Alawad. THE WESTERN BAHR AL-GHAZAL UNDER BRITISH RULE: 1898-1956. 1991. 183pp.
161-6 $15.00*

Latin America Series

8. Clayton, Lawrence A. CAULKERS AND CARPENTERS IN A NEW WORLD: The Shipyards of Colonial Guayaquil. 1980. 189pp., illus.
103-9 $15.00*

9. Tata, Robert J. STRUCTURAL CHANGES IN PUERTO RICO'S ECONOMY: 1947-1976. 1981. xiv, 104pp.
107-1 $12.00*

11. O'Shaughnessy, Laura N., and Louis H. Serra. CHURCH AND REVOLUTION IN NICARAGUA. 1986. 118pp.
126-8 $12.00*

12. Wallace, Brian. OWNERSHIP AND DEVELOPMENT: A Comparison of Domestic and Foreign Investment in Columbian Manufacturing. 1987. 186pp.
145-4 $10.00*

13. Henderson, James D. CONSERVATIVE THOUGHT IN LATIN AMERICA: The Ideas of Laureano Gomez. 1988. 150pp.
148-9 $13.00*

14. Summ, G. Harvey, and Tom Kelly. THE GOOD NEIGHBORS: America, Panama, and the 1977 Canal Treaties. 1988. 135pp.
149-7 $13.00*

15. Peritore, Patrick. SOCIALISM, COMMUNISM, AND LIBERATION THEOLOGY IN BRAZIL: An Opinion Survey Using Q-Methodology. 1990. 245pp.
156-X   15.00*

Southeast Asia Series

31. Nash, Manning. PEASANT CITIZENS: Politics, Religion, and Modernization in Kelantan, Malaysia. 1974. 181pp.
018-0 $12.00*

38. Bailey, Conner. BROKER, MEDIATOR, PATRON, AND KINSMAN: An Historical Analysis of Key Leadership Roles in a Rural Malaysian District. 1976. 79pp.
024-5 $ 8.00*

44. Collier, William L., et al. INCOME, EMPLOYMENT AND FOOD SYSTEMS IN JAVANESE COASTAL VILLAGES. 1977. 160pp.
031-8 $10.00*

45. Chew, Sock Foon and MacDougall, John A. FOREVER PLURAL: The Perception and Practice of Inter-Communal Marriage in Singapore. 1977. 61pp.
030-X $ 8.00*

47. Wessing, Robert. COSMOLOGY AND SOCIAL BEHAVIOR IN A WEST JAVANESE SETTLEMENT. 1978. 200pp.
072-5 $12.00*

48. Willer, Thomas F., ed. SOUTHEAST ASIAN REFER-
ENCES IN THE BRITISH PARLIAMENTARY PAPERS,
1801-1972/73: An Index. 1978. 110pp.
033-4 $ 8.50*

49. Durrenberger, E. Paul. AGRICULTURAL PRODUCTION
AND HOUSEHOLD BUDGETS IN A SHAN PEASANT
VILLAGE IN NORTHWESTERN THAILAND: A Quanti-
tative Description. 1978. 142pp.
071-7 $10.00*

50. Echauz, Robustiano. SKETCHES OF THE ISLAND OF
NEGROS. 1978. 174pp.
070-9 $12.00*

51. Krannich, Ronald L. MAYORS AND MANAGERS IN
THAILAND: The Struggle for Political Life in Administrative
Settings. 1978. 139pp.
073-3 $11.00*

56A. Duiker, William J. VIETNAM SINCE THE FALL OF
SAIGON. Updated edition. 1989. 383pp.
162-4 $17.00*

59. Foster, Brian L. COMMERCE AND ETHNIC DIFFER-
ENCES: The Case of the Mons in Thailand. 1982. x, 93pp.
112-8 $10.00*

60. Frederick, William H., and John H. McGlynn.
REFLECTIONS ON REBELLION: Stories from the
Indonesian Upheavals of 1948 and 1965. 1983. vi, 168pp.
111-X $ 9.00*

61. Cady, John F. CONTACTS WITH BURMA, 1935-1949: A
Personal Account. 1983. x, 117pp.
114-4 $ 9.00*

63. Carstens, Sharon, ed. CULTURAL IDENTITY IN
NORTHERN PENINSULAR MALAYSIA. 1986. 91pp.
116-0 $ 9.00*

64. Dardjowidjojo, Soenjono. VOCABULARY BUILDING IN INDONESIAN: An Advanced Reader. 1984. xviii, 256pp.
118-7 $26.00*

65. Errington, J. Joseph. LANGUAGE AND SOCIAL CHANGE IN JAVA: Linguistic Reflexes of Modernization in a Traditional Royal Polity. 1985. xiv, 198pp.
120-9 $12.00*

66. Binh, Tran Tu. THE RED EARTH: A Vietnamese Memoir of Life on a Colonial Rubber Plantation. Tr. by John Spragens. Ed. by David Marr. 1985. xii, 98pp.
119-5 $11.00*

68. Syukri, Ibrahim. HISTORY OF THE MALAY KINGDOM OF PATANI. Tr. by Conner Bailey and John N. Miksic. 1985. xix, 113pp.
123-3 $12.00*

69. Keeler, Ward. JAVANESE: A Cultural Approach. 1984. xxxvi, 523pp.
121-7 $18.00*

70. Wilson, Constance M., and Lucien M. Hanks. BURMA-THAILAND FRONTIER OVER SIXTEEN DECADES: Three Descriptive Documents. 1985. x, 128pp.
124-1 $11.00*

71. Thomas, Lynn L., and Franz von Benda-Beckmann, eds. CHANGE AND CONTINUITY IN MINANGKABAU: Local, Regional, and Historical Perspectives on West Sumatra. 1986. 363pp.
127-6 $16.00*

72. Reid, Anthony, and Oki Akira, eds. THE JAPANESE EXPERIENCE IN INDONESIA: Selected Memoirs of 1942-1945. 1986. 411pp., 20 illus.
132-2 $20.00*

73. Smirenskaia, Zhanna D. PEASANTS IN ASIA: Social Consciousness and Social Struggle. Tr. by Michael J. Buckley. 1987. 248pp.
134-9 $14.00

74. McArthur, M.S.H. REPORT ON BRUNEI IN 1904. Ed. by A.V.M. Horton. 1987. 304pp.
135-7 $15.00

75. Lockard, Craig Alan. FROM KAMPUNG TO CITY. A Social History of Kuching Malaysia 1820-1970. 1987. 311pp.
136-5 $16.00*

76. McGinn, Richard. STUDIES IN AUSTRONESIAN LINGUISTICS. 1988. 492pp.
137-3 $20.00*

77. Muego, Benjamin N. SPECTATOR SOCIETY: The Philippines Under Martial Rule. 1988. 232pp.
138-1 $15.00*

78. Chew, Sock Foon. ETHNICITY AND NATIONALITY IN SINGAPORE. 1987. 229pp.
139-X $12.50*

79. Walton, Susan Pratt. MODE IN JAVANESE MUSIC. 1987. 279pp.
144-6 $15.00*

80. Nguyen Anh Tuan. SOUTH VIETNAM TRIAL AND EXPERIENCE: A Challenge for Development. 1987. 482pp.
141-1 $18.00*

81. Van der Veur, Paul W., ed. TOWARD A GLORIOUS INDONESIA: Reminiscences and Observations of Dr. Soetomo. 1987. 367pp.
142-X $16.00*

82. Spores, John C. RUNNING AMOK: An Historical Inquiry. 1988. 190pp.
   140-3 $14.00*

83. Tan Malaka. FROM JAIL TO JAIL. Tr. and ed. by Helen Jarvis. 1990. 3 vols. 1,226pp.
   150-0 $45.00*

84. Devas, Nick. FINANCING LOCAL GOVERNMENT IN INDONESIA. 1989. 344pp.
   153-5 $16.00*

85. Suryadinata, Leo. MILITARY ASCENDANCY AND POLITICAL CULTURE: A Study of Indonesia's Golkar. 1989. 222pp.
   179-9 $15.00*

86. Williams, Michael. COMMUNISM, RELIGION, AND REVOLT IN BANTEN. 1990. 356pp.
   155-1 $16.00*

87. Hudak, Thomas John. THE INDIGENIZATION OF PALI METERS IN THAI POETRY. 1990. 237pp.
   159-4 $15.00*

ORDERING INFORMATION

Orders for titles in the Monographs in International Studies series should be placed through the Ohio University Press/Scott Quadrangle/Athens, Ohio 45701-2979, USA. Individuals must remit pre-payment via check, VISA, MasterCard, CHOICE, or American Express. Individuals ordering from the United Kingdom, Continental Europe, Middle East, and Africa should order through Academic and University Publishers Group, 1 Gower Street, London WC1E 6HA, England. Orders from the Pacific Region, Asia, Australia, and New Zealand should be sent to East-West Export Books, c/o The University of Hawaii Press, 2840 Kolowalu Street, Honolulu, Hawaii 96822, USA.

Other individuals ordering from outside of the U.S., please remit in U.S. funds by either International Money Order or check drawn on a U.S. bank. Postage and handling is $3.00 for the first book and $1.00 for each additional book. Prices and availability are subject to change without notice.

Out-of-print titles may be ordered from University Microfilms, Inc., 300 North Zeeb Road, Ann Arbor, Michigan 48106, USA.